America's Greatest National Disaster

America's Greatest National Disaster

President Donald J. Trump

Bobby E. Mills, PhD

CONTENTS

Acknowledgments

The chaos of the 2016 Republican Party primary and the subsequent election of Donald J. Trump to the office of president has proven to be America's greatest national disaster. Former Governor Jeb Bush called Donald J. Trump the "CHAOS" candidate and now he is the "CHAOS" President. In the past, America has experienced numerous "natural" disasters, but the presence of Donald J. Trump in The White House is having horrific negative consequences for the entire world community.

On the one hand, it is natural for an individual to love himself/herself. But, on the other hand, it is unnatural for an individual to be *in love* with himself/herself. President Trump's behavior is a clear indicator that he is in love with Donald J. Trump, not America. Hence, it is extremely difficult for him to love the American people or the founding democratic Constitutional principles upon which the USA is established. In fact, President Trump is seeking to revisit the Civil War. For after all, in his heart and mind, he does not have room for anyone else, especially minorities. Love is an outward expression of the inward reality of God simply because God is LOVE. "For God so loved the world, that he gave his only begotten Son, that whosoever believeth in him should not perish, but have everlasting life" (John 3:16).

Unfortunately, there will always be at least thirty-three percent of the American voting population that will absolutely love the Donald Trumps of America, because they hate God, themselves, and more importantly, they hate what America constitutionally represents: "We hold these truths to be self-evident, that all men are created equal, that they are endowed by their Creator with certain unalienable Rights, that among these are Life, Liberty, and the Pursuit of Happiness..." Without a doubt, Christian evangelicals who claim to love God and, at the same time, throw bricks of hatred at God's creation and hide their hands. The Bible writer Paul states it clearly: "Professing themselves to be wise, they became fools, and changed the glory of the uncorruptible God into an image made like corruptible man [Donald J. Trump]" (Romans 1:22). America, "There is no wisdom nor understanding nor counsel against the Lord" (Proverbs 21:30). Beware, Christian evangelicals, "Thou hypocrite, first cast out the beam out of thine own eye; and then shalt thou see clearly to cast out the mote out of thy brother's eye" (Matthew 7:5). America, trust God because this too shall pass!

I thank my family for their loving support, especially my wife, Larnita, for her positive critique of my thoughts, my son Daryl Anthony, and my daughters Kelly Leigh and Karen Mills Richardson. Grateful appreciation and heartfelt thanks to Charles W. Moore, Pastor Robert E. Childress, Pastor Raymond L. Farley, Pastor John E. Cameron, and Dr. Etta F. Walker for their spiritual-based friendship over the years. To God be the glory. I love and thank you all in Jesus' name. Selah!

INTRODUCTION

Let's be absolutely clear about why Donald J. Trump won the 2016 presidential election and why Hillary Clinton lost. The outcome of the 2016 presidential election can only be explained by one overriding ungodly factor: racism. Racism was displayed at its highest level prior to the 1964-1965 Civil Rights Act and Voting Rights Act. But, beyond a shadow of a doubt, race still matters in American society. Institutional racism, racist-oriented Christian Evangelicals, and spiritually-morally confused working class individuals elected Donald J. Trump to the office of president. It was not lack of jobs, trade agreements, or any other economic factors; it was unadulterated racism in all of its vulgar forms. In fact, President Trump was given a spiritual-moral-leadership test concerning the ungodliness of racism on Saturday, August 12th, 2017. He failed the test, because morally and culturally the presidency plays a different kind of moral role in American society other than just partisan politics. President Trump was and is spiritually and morally unprepared to lead.

The Trump campaign slogan, "Make America Great (White) Again," awakened the evil forces of institutional racism, not lack of employment opportunities. Without a doubt, there are serious consequences to this type of exclusionary devilish thinking, especially in a democratic society. For after all, racism engenders insanity. For example, during the Republican Party primary, Donald J. Trump declared that he could "shoot someone on Fifth Avenue and his loyal supporters would still support him." WHY? Or he could assault a woman by grabbing her private anatomy and she would love it, because he is multi-billionaire. If this is not the epitome of insanity, then what is insanity? Additionally, President Trump was the driving force with Republican Party primary voters behind the "birther movement." Let's assume for the sake of argument that Barack Obama was born in Africa (Kenya) to an American (mother) citizen and an African father. Senator Ted Cruz was born in Canada to an American (mother) citizen and a Cuban father. Question: What is the difference? Think about it! One is eligible and acceptable as President and one is not. WHY?

By the way, individuals who practice (espouse) racism have a God Complex problem in conjunction with a personal self-identity problem. Behold the words of the Prophet Jeremiah: "Before I formed thee in the belly I knew thee, and before thou camest forth out of the womb I sanctified thee" (Jeremiah 1:5). For after all, even Donald J. Trump is one of God's creations. Hence, God hates racism. Moreover, God is the source of human life. And, "God judgeth the righteous, and God is angry with the wicked every day" (Psalm 7:11). This applies even to President Trump as well as his Christian Evangelical supporters. Somewhere I read that God made a man (Adam) from the dirt. Maybe this is why the oldest origin of human skeleton life was discovered in Africa as the remains of "Lucy."

Hence, to describe the news as "fake" in a democratic society, where a free press is an important cornerstone of democracy, is also insanity as well as a lack of spiritual-moral conscience. "The Lord gave the word: great was the company of those that published it" (Psalm 68:11). A free press is an important cornerstone in a social democracy.

President Trump does not understand that America is 5% of the world's population, but we control 20% of the world's economy. Free trade is an important factor in the economic well-being (development) of American society. Since the 1930's, America has been the dominant economic force in the world community. Above all, America is a nation of immigrations, and therefore, immigration is a central cultural feature as well as an important economic dimension of American society. Referring to immigrants as "aliens" is a counter-productive nation building strategy. Immigrants do not come from another planet. And, at the same time, all Americans understand what is wrong with illegal immigration—it is illegal.

The Russians wanted democracy to equal chaos, just as their so-called democracy equals chaos in Russia. Apparently, to some degree, with President Trump in the White House, the goal was accomplished. For after all, political and economic power in Russia is in the hands of one man: Putin. President Trump, in the state of West Virginia, declared that the Russians did not help him win the presidency. The Russian hacking of the Democratic National Committee (DNC) as well as John Podesta's (Clinton's campaign manager) email account confused individuals who were already spiritually-morally confused. Of course, given his behavior in the Republican Party primary, considering voting for Donald J. Trump as President of the United States of America, in and of itself was an act of confusion. The Russians even hacked this writer's email account because of social commentaries regarding the 2016 election of Donald J. Trump. I was given this information by the proper legal authorities concerning who hacked my computer system. Seventeen different national security agencies have certified that the Russians attempted to tilt America's democratic election in the favor of Donald J. Trump as their candidate for President. Why? This is why there is an on-going investigation to find out the why of it all.

There are four overriding reasons why Hillary Clinton lost the 2016 presidential election:

- The entrance of Senator Bernie Sanders into the 2016 Democratic Party primary process as a Democrat, although he was an Independent, created untold confusion simply because he had a built-in electoral base of Independent voters. Moreover, in the past, Democratic candidates have had to earn the Independent vote. Senator Sanders had already earned the Independent vote because he was an Independent.

- Unfortunately, Independents tend to believe most of the Republican propaganda about Democrats, and at the same time, embrace very little of the racist-oriented reality of Republican Party polices. Consequently, in the general election Independents have a tendency to not vote in the general election, especially if their particular candidate loses in the primary process. Democrats can remedy this issue by establishing a policy procedure that an individual must declare four years in advance that he/she will seek the Democratic Party presidential primary nomination.

- The Obama Factor: A two-term president and his blackness. The devilish and sinful desire on the part of Republican Party officials to erase the historic contributions of the Obama presidency. Questions: Can you erase 20 million Americans that received health insurance under the Obama Presidency? Can you eliminate the threat of Osama Bin Laden? Moreover, the congeniality that existed between the Obamas and Hillary Clinton—at least thirty-three percent of white America could not accept that level of respect between black and white with an emphasis on a black man and a black woman helping a white woman become the first female president.

- Christian evangelicals and the race factor utilizing Donald J. Trump's battle-cry: "Make America Great (White) Again". In other words, it is time to "put minorities back in their place again." After 1964 and 1965, America made great strides toward equality and justice for all under the law. President Trump in conjunction with alt-right (white) nationalists and Christian evangelicals via Christian churches is orchestrating racial division in American society in the name of God. Christian evangelicals, when given a spiritual-moral choice, chose Barabbas. Choices have consequences. If, in the twinkling of an eye, you hear the *boom* and you think it is thunder, and the sky lights up with fury and fire, it means goodbye. So what if we destroy North Korea? What is North Korea? A failed nation-state that cannot feed itself! "Fools rush in where angels fail to tread." America, all of this insanity is absolutely uncalled for, because one insane man is talking to another insane man, and of course, neither one know what to do. This indeed is a sad socio-spiritual commentary for a great nation-state such as America. Let's not lose the little spiritual consciousness that we do have as a nation state. For it is said, "Be not deceived: evil communications corrupt good manners" (1 Corinthians 15:33). America, you know full well, that "fools make a mock at sin: but among the righteous there is favor" (Proverbs 14:9). Christian evangelicals, maybe this is why President Donald J. Trump does not attend church services.

With the election of Donald J. Trump, the Republican Party as well as American society lost their soul, and the following scripture will shed spiritual light on why: America is neither sober nor vigilant in the things of God. "Be sober, be vigilant; because your adversary the devil [North Korea and Russia], as a roaring lion, walketh about, seeking whom he may devour: whom resist steadfast in the faith, knowing that the same afflictions are accomplished in your brethren that are in the world" (1 Peter 5:8-9). Previous presidents knew how to be sober minded, vigilant, and above all, understand the military might of America's military system by "being still and watching the salvation of the Lord."

America, let's fervently always pray this thought-provoking prayer: "Almighty God, Father of our Lord Jesus Christ, maker of all things, judge of all men: We acknowledge and bewail our manifold sins and wickedness, which from time to time, most grievously have we committed, by thought, word, and deed, against thy divine majesty. We do earnestly repent, and are heartily sorry for these our misdoings; the remembrance of them is grievous unto us. Have mercy upon us, have mercy upon us, most merciful Father. For thy Son our Lord Jesus Christ's sake, forgive us all that is past; and grant that we may ever hereafter serve and please thee in newness of life, to the honor and glory of thy name; through Jesus Christ our Lord. Amen."

To God be the glory for the things He has done. Selah!

PRESIDENT DONALD J. TRUMP: GOD'S PERMISSIVE WILL!

God has a permissive will and God has a sovereign will. Donald J. Trump becoming the 45th President of these United States of America was indeed God's permissive will, not his sovereign will. God's sovereign will is based solely upon God's principles, and God does not violate his sovereign/sacred principles of primary reference. God gave Moses his sovereign will at the burning bush on Mount Sinai, enshrined later as The Ten Commandments or The Law.

American society is spiritually and morally upside-down because too many religious and political leaders have strayed from God's sovereign will, precepts, and principles in search of power and money: material empire building versus kingdom of God building. As a result, the principles and precepts of God are not in the equation—only material empire building. Behold, forewarned is foretold: all it takes for the world to get off-course (off-track) is for good men and good women to be silent and do nothing. Herein is the central problem in the Grand Ole Party (Republican Party): Only a few good men will stand up and speak out, for example, Senator John McCain. Moreover, we all know: "For with the heart man believeth unto righteousness; and with the mouth confession is made unto salvation" (Romans 10:10). America, nations rise and nations fall, and even, "heaven and earth shall pass away, but my words shall not pass away"

(Matthew 24:35).

Presently, American society is the bastion of social democracy. The spiritual beauty of American social democracy is its professed desire to create a godly, just, equalitarian society as expressed in the preamble to the U.S. Constitution. In fact, the Preamble to the U.S. Constitution is a powerful spiritual declaration: "We hold these Truths to be self-evident, that all men are created equal, that they are endowed by their Creator with certain unalienable Rights, that among these are Life, Liberty, and the Pursuit of Happiness." This is why voting is sacred and extremely important in American culture. Voting is the foundational symbol of equalitarian citizenship, especially in the selection and election of political leaders—the principle of "one person, one vote". This is the only logical explanation for why Blacks were systematically denied voting rights prior to the 1964 Civil Rights Act and the 1965 Voting Rights Act.

Since Adam and Eve in the Garden of Eden, both men as well as women have been violating God's sovereign will based upon God's gift of free will (choice). Life is about choices. Choices have consequences, both positive and negative. For God so loved us that he did not make human beings automatons that are programmed simply to do His Will as robots without choice.

America proclaims that she is one nation formed out of many different cultures. To be sure, because of the track record and ungodly mentality of Donald J. Trump as well as the self-serving mentality of his co-conspirators, Christian Evangelicals, we can't get anywhere near the sacred, holy, godlike place of a democratic nation of equals. President Trump cannot help America become one out of many. Without a doubt, "When he speaketh fair, believe him not: for there are seven abominations in his heart" (Proverbs 26:25). Therefore, the election of President Trump was indeed a rejection of moral order in American society. In fact, Trump's election parallels the desire of Israel for a King and not the spiritual-moral order of God. Based upon the electoral college system, America desired an immoral, crooked businessman (money), rather than spiritual-moral order. The 45th President of these United States of America was and is a democratic institution destroyer.

For example, from Holy Scripture it is self-evident that the Prophet Samuel was God's anointed (sovereign will leader) for the people of Israel. But, Israel wanted a secular-minded king in order to be like other nations. God told Samuel to tell the people of Israel: A (king) will take your sons and daughters. "But the thing displeased Samuel, when they said, Give us a King to judge us. And Samuel prayed unto the Lord. And the Lord said unto Samuel, Hearken unto the voice of the people in all that they say unto thee: for they have not rejected thee, but they have rejected me, that I should not reign over them" (1 Samuel 8:6-7). In voting for Donald J. Trump, did America reject God? We all know that Christian Evangelicals are brazen hypocrites! But, are the Christian Evangelical supporters of Donald J. Trump secular-minded, as well? "Professing themselves to be wise, they became fools, and changed the glory of the uncorruptible God into an image made like to corruptible man" (Romans 1:22-23).

Can American society survive the ungodly, immoral, mentality of a President Donald J. Trump in The White House, especially since he has broad-based Christian Evangelical support? America, as Samuel told the Israelites, the king will take your sons and daughters. Likewise, President Donald J. Trump is preparing to embark upon taking your sons and daughters through mission creep in Afghanistan! America, understand history: Afghanistan is an unwinnable war as was Viet Nam.

Every individual should embark upon a search for God because death is a certainty; and, one glorious day, each and every individual will meet God face to face. "It is appointed unto men once to die, but after this judgment" (Hebrews 9:27). Unfortunately, President Trump has enslaved the Republican Party to the vanity of lies, not the reality of GOD and truth. Moreover, President Trump has enslaved the Republican Party into a vulgar search for power and money rather than the truth and reality of God. President Lyndon B. Johnson had it right: a "great society" takes care of the least among us. Jesus declared, "Then shall the righteous answer him, saying, Lord, when saw we thee an hungered, and fed thee? Or thirsty, and gave thee drink? When saw we thee a stranger, and took thee in? or naked, and clothed thee? Or when saw we thee sick, or in prison, and came unto thee? And the King shall answer and say unto them, Verily I say unto you, Inasmuch as ye have done it unto the least of these my brethren, ye have done it unto me" (Matthew 25:37-40). Selah!

If It Must Be: It Shall Be!

To be for the sake of being is not a reason in the greatest social democracy on the face of the earth. One of the greatest poets, Alfred Lord Tennyson, said it best: "Ours not to reason why, ours but to do and die." Tennyson was absolutely correct only about spiritual things, because individuals die regardless of whether they want to or not. "And as it is appointed unto men once to die, but after this the judgment" (Hebrews 9:27). Judgment is spiritual. "God judgeth the righteous, and God is angry with the wicked every day" (Psalm 7:11). For after all, we are in the "Age-Of-Trump-Doctrine" (TRUMPDOM) and every American must believe that "the house of the wicked shall be overthrown: but the tabernacle of the upright shall flourish." (Proverbs 14: 12). Apparently, President Trump believes in doing evil for the sake of doing evil simply because of lack of God consciousness and to establish a New World Order, which in turn, would be disastrous for the world.

However, Tennyson was absolutely incorrect about flesh-oriented things and the material world. Individuals should never choose to die for immoral reasons/causes, only choose to die for a just cause. Moreover, it is a personal decision that is only in the heart and mind of the individual who chooses to place his life on the line. Of course, only God can judge individual motive and this is why an individual can do the right thing from the wrong motive, and it is SIN.

America, let's be perfectly clear about why Donald J. Trump was elected President of the greatest social democracy in the world. Coded racist phrases and latent racism elected Trump to The White House in conjunction with "bhite backlash" because of the election of Barack Obama as a two-term President. Also let us be clear about why America's democratic institutions are being assaulted. Make no mistake about it: American social democracy and America's leadership in the free world is being trashed by the Trump Administration. President Trump used coded language to White males and some White females in order to galvanize their votes, and it was successful. Currently, America is not imperiled by trade agreements, job losses, or socio-economic-political influences in the free world. The external threats to America's democratic influence in the world community are Russia, China, North Korea and Iran. However, there are greater socio-spiritual internal threats to America's well-being, because it is those threats that produced the election of Donald J. Trump to the Office of President. Evangelicals, there are consequences in your vote (chaos, confusion, and misuse of governmental resources). You must now own the societal consequences of your spiritual vote. Christian Right Evangelical pastoral leaders, God is beseeching you: "therefore, brethren, by the mercies of God, that ye present your bodies a living sacrifice, holy, acceptable unto God, which is your reasonable service. And be not conformed to this world: but be ye transformed by the renewing of your mind, that ye may prove what is that good, and acceptable, and perfect will of God (Romans 12:1-2). By the way, Donald J. Trump emphatically told you that he could not come anywhere near any of these spiritual precepts. And, you still voted for a merciless, confused, uncaring individual that told you he could "shoot someone on Fifth

Avenue and you would still support him." Hypocrites, hypocrites, and hypocrites! "Thou hypocrite, first cast out the beam that is in thine own eye; and then shalt thou see clearly to cast out the mote out of thy brother's eye" (Matthew 7:5). More importantly, pastoral leaders preach and espouse the Gospel of Jesus Christ, and above all, preach the truth about race and stop preaching personalized-isms. "Isms" create schisms, which in turn, are not of God. God hates racism. Racism creates insanity, and without a doubt, America has governing insanity going on in The White House. In fact, in recent national polling data it has been empirically documented that the level of racism in American society was underestimated by most god-fearing Americans.

Donald J. Trump told the American people in no uncertain terms the unadulterated truth about himself, which in turn, was mostly evil. Love is an outward expression of an internal spiritual reality (GOD). Love is about giving, not self-centered ego-taking; "EGO" is an acronym for "Edge God Out." Initially, there were (613) commandments and most individuals could not live by them. God condensed them to 10 on Mt. Sinai and most individuals could not live by them. A lawyer dealing the power of technicality asked Jesus a question, tempting him, and saying, "Master, which is the greatest Commandment in the law? Jesus said unto him, Thou shalt love the Lord thy God with all thy heart, and with all thy soul, and with all thy mind. This is the first and great commandment. And the second is like unto it, Thou shalt love thy neighbor as thyself. On these two commandments hang all the law and the prophets" (Matthew 22:37-40). Christian Right Evangelicals, this is a profound spiritual lesson that President Trump evidently never learned, because he certainly does not practice it. Trump's commandment is the "I" syndrome that is the "I" that is smack-dab in the middle of SIN. It is, indeed, unfortunate because it seems as though 80 percent of Christian Right Evangelicals who supported Trump did not learn this spiritual lesson either. Obviously, individuals cannot teach with spiritual fervor that which they do not believe. America, President Trump's leadership behavior suggests that he indeed does not know anything about the Love of God, love for Country, or positive love for self. Moreover, when individuals do not understand this spiritual fact of life you are already in HELL, and your only choice is to create HELL for others. America, "In God We Trust"; and those who trust in President Trump know full well that he is creating "HELL" in America.

Moreover, some White men consistently lied on Hillary Clinton, and absolutely nothing criminal was ever proven (under-oath) after numerous congressional investigations and hearings. All of this partisan-political nonsense for White Privilege produced nothing in spite of Republicans being in charge of both the House and the Senate. But, more importantly, Senators Collins and Murkowski are profound socio-spiritual examples of why America just might need more women in politics rather than fewer. Finally, America, there are two spiritual traits that an individual must possess in order for God to entrust him/her with a godly mission: "And the Lord said unto Moses, I will do this thing also that thou hast spoken: for thou hast found grace in my sight, and I know thee by name" (Exodus 33:17). God does not know everybody by name.

Christian Right Evangelicals, does God know President Donald J. Trump by name? Selah!

O.J. Simpson: President Donald J. Trump

America, we are in a hellish sinful immoral national state of being for many and varied reasons, but primarily because of racism. Far too many White males want Black males to apologize for being Black. Just a divine reminder, Black males had no choice in their skin color. Likewise, White males have no choice in their skin color. God is the designer of skin color, not human beings. Moreover, individuals that have a skin color problem invariably have a God problem. Without a doubt, the majority of Blacks in America give no place to the devil, because the devil is the author of confusion. "Be ye angry, and sin not: let not the sun go down upon your wrath: neither give place to the devil" (Ephesians 4:26). Therefore, Christian Evangelicals know full well: "For God is not the author of confusion, but of peace, as in all churches of the saints" (1 Corinthians 14:33). To be sure, Black men have always been godly proud; and, consequently, through and by the mercies of Almighty God, have been able to transcend many of the obstacles of institutional racism.

An individual becoming lifted-up in pride is the epitome of devilishness. Again, this is why the Bible declares, "Be ye angry, and sin not: let not the sun go down upon your wrath: neither give place to the devil" (Ephesians 4:27).

O.J. Simpson and President Donald J. Trump are flip-sides of the same coin. O.J. beat the system in the court room by following the rules and procedures of the system with high powered lawyers. Now, they can't get over it. What O. J. experienced is something that rarely, if ever, happens for any Black man: Justice in a courtroom. For after all, the average Black man is guilty when arrested; and, therefore, simply goes through a court process before the day of confinement or execution is announced. No one is absolutely certain of O. J. Simpson's guilt, because the system declared him innocent. But, we do know that because he was accused of murdering two White individuals in the minds of most Whites, O.J. is as guilty as sin!

On the other hand, President Donald J. Trump is destroying America's democratic institutions with lies. Lies and President Trump go together like hand and glove. President Trump does have some assistance from some Republican Party officials who lack moral objectivity or intellectual integrity. It seems as though most Republicans are Republicans before they are Americans, that is, they place party loyalty above national interests. President Trump will throw anyone and everyone not under the bus, but on the railroad tracks in order that the train crushes them to death. Ask Jeff Sessions, a loyalist to the nth degree, regardless of right or wrong. In the final analysis, history will not be kind to Republican Party loyalists who have placed partisan politics (power and money) above democratic national interests.

America and its NATO allies must realize what it is that President Trump, in a vulgar fashion, is attempting to do in conjunction with Russia as co-conspirators: establish a new world order. Strange bedfellows produce strange politics as well as fruit. America, know full well, "As I live, saith the Lord, every knee shall bow to me, and every tongue shall confess to God. So then every one of us shall give an account of himself to God" (Romans 14:11-12). Life is about choices and accountability. Therefore, America, stand up, speak out, and, above all, tell the truth, the whole truth, and nothing but the truth so help you God. And, know full well, that there is no such animal as a little white lie.

Most Americans believe that O.J. Simpson is guilty of a double murder. However, this we do fully know, in order to remain as President of these United States of America, Trump will initiate a war to remain in office and to be reelected in 2020. Behold, the Trump war time cabinet. In fact, President Trump will destroy your sons and daughters because of his insatiable EGO (Edge God Out). Most Americans can walk away from power when their very soul is imperiled; even Sean Spicer was able to walk away, but not Jeff Sessions. America, President Trump is a man that cannot walk away from power and privilege because of his dictatorial personality. Remember, Trump loyalists, the road to hell is paved with good intentions. By the way, at the end of the day, good and moral actions are what really matters, not good intentions.

Let's be perfectly clear about this: "power corrupts and absolute power corrupts absolutely." Please, Christian Evangelicals, run this scripture past President Trump for his spiritual edification. "Take heed, and beware of covetousness: for a man's life consisteth not in the abundance of the things which he possesseth" (Luke 12:15). And, after introducing President Trump to this scripture, reintroduce yourselves to this scriptural verse of inspiration: "For what shall it profit a man, if he shall gain the whole world, and lose his own soul? Or what shall a man give in exchange for his soul" (Luke 8:36-37). It appears as though President Trump will give anything and everything in order to become co-leader of the world with Putin. However, in the final analysis, they will be plotting against each other, because that is what dictators do.

America, God is a promise-keeper, not a promise-breaker. Moreover, God has promised us life and life more abundantly, if we "but seek ye first the Kingdom of God, and his righteousness; and all these things shall be added unto you" (Matthew 6:33). God has already made provision for us, if we are obedient to his word. Therefore, we do not need to thingify ourselves by loving things. Because, "Whereby are given unto us exceeding great and precious promises: that by these ye might be partakers of the divine nature, having escaped the corruption that is in the world through lust" (2 Peter 1: 4).

Both O. J. Simpson and President Trump have played the system, especially by beating the odds to their personal and professional advantages. O. J., in a criminal court room, with high-powered defense attorneys, and by "pulling a rabbit out of a hat," was found not guilty of murder. President Trump, in bankruptcy courts, with high-powered corporate attorneys stiffing small businessmen—four bankruptcies. Not to mention the assistance of Russian hacking in the 2016 Presidential election. Lest we forget, the disdain that some Whites had and still have for the election of the first Black President as well as a woman being in the Presidential leadership position. Selah!

Organized Chaos Is Still Chaos

Chaos by any other name is still chaos. The Trump Administration is publicly attempting to micro-manage chaos through lying and creating more chaos. The best approach to managing chaos is to not create it. For example, the Trump Administration is attempting to create chaos in America's democratic voting process by claiming that there is wide-spread voter fraud. Without a doubt, American social democracy does not have a voter fraud problem. America has a malnutrition of the brain leadership problem. Christian Evangelicals and most White men have accepted chaos as normal when it is abnormal. For after all, there is nothing normal about what the Trump Administration is doing. Question: Why do they love it? Does the answer lie in self-hatred? Does the answer lie in their inability to experience Ultimate Reality (God) and spirituality? Or does the answer lie in their inability to achieve physical and material success unless through White Privilege?

Let's be perfectly clear about self-hatred and its origin. Is the origin family socialization and societal cultural adaptation? Societal hatred toward minority groups is not embedded in the Preamble to the U.S Constitution nor the Articles of the Constitution. "For the wrath of God is revealed from heaven against all ungodliness and unrighteousness of men, who hold the truth in unrighteousness; because that which may be known of God is manifest in them; for God hath shewed it unto them. For the invisible things of him from the creation of the world are clearly seen, being understood by the things that are made, even his eternal power and Godhead; so that they are without excuse" (Romans 1:18-20). However, man-made law is simply this: "Ignorance of the LAW is no excuse." Unfortunately, the Trump family, Trump White House Administration, and Christian Evangelicals make excuse after excuse for their ungodliness and complete disrespect for constitutional law.

American society is the bastion of freedom in the world community, especially among democratic nation-states. However, under the leadership of President Trump less so, simply because of his dictatorial personality traits of "my way or the highway." Trump and Putin are hell-bent on creating a new world order based upon ungodliness and brute power. "For, brethren, ye have been called unto liberty; only use not liberty for an occasion to the flesh, but by love serve one another" (Galatians 5:13). President Trump, as well as Russian Dictator Putin, are hell-bent on enslaving the world to the pleasures of the flesh. Christian Evangelicals, "There is therefore now no condemnation to them which are in Christ Jesus, who walk not after the flesh, but after the Spirit. For the law of the Spirit of life in Christ Jesus hath made me free from the law of sin and death. For what the law could not do, in that it was weak through the flesh, God sending his own Son in the likeness of sinful flesh, and for sin, condemned sin in the flesh: that the righteousness of the law might be fulfilled in us, who walk not after the flesh, but after the Spirit." (Romans 8:2-4). Now, we all know why President Trump never or rarely ever attends church services: lack of spiritual conscience. Of course, Christian Evangelicals attend church services every Sunday and, at the same time, appear not to have a spiritual conscience. "Can two walk together, except they be agreed?" (Amos 3:3). America, pray that Christian Evangelicals know what God requires: "He hath shewed thee, O man, what is good; and what doth the Lord require of thee, but to do justly, and to love mercy, and to walk humbly with thy God" (Micah 6:8).

Christian Evangelicals, please inform Donald J. Trump that the U.S. Presidency is a higher calling to public service, not personalized family business deal making. The primary reason for Donald J. Trump's election is that too many Americans are using their freedom to serve the vanity of the flesh rather than serving each other in the Spirit of God "Thou shalt love thy neighbor as thyself" (Matthew 22:39).

What transforms a collection of individuals and families into a nation is the will to create a just society based upon democratic principles of institutional-ethical fairness, because justice is a spiritual concept. Therefore, justice should be in the court-room, not in the halls (halls of justice). If all that is being said is not enough to change America's (direction) from that of being a nation of pathetic, pleasure-seeking hypocrites to "one nation under God with liberty and justice for all," God help us! For we all know that "The steps of a good man are ordered by the Lord: and he delighted in his way" (Psalms 37:23). The world knows that President Trump and President Putin are not good or godly men, and every American ought to know, as well. In fact, every American should know: "Be not deceived; God is not mocked: for whatsoever a man soweth, that shall he also reap. For he that soweth to his flesh shall of his flesh reap corruption; but he that soweth to the Spirit shall of the Spirit reap life everlasting" (Galatians 6:7-8).

A lot of conflict of interests concerns could easily be "cleared-up" if President Trump would simply release his federal income tax returns; and, therefore, every American would, without a doubt, know who he truly serves—country or self/family. For after all, who is it that President Trump is attempting to make great? Country or self? But, more importantly, the moral inconsistency of Republican Party officials is woefully shameful, because of their blind-eyed, power play, money grapping complicity in the destruction of America's democratic institutions. "Therefore leaving the principles of the doctrine of Christ, let us go on unto perfection; not laying again the foundation of repentance from dead works, and of faith toward God, And this will we do, if God permit" (Hebrews 6:1-3). Selah!

Ungodly Words Incite Devilish Deadly Actions

"Death and life are in the power of the tongue:" (Proverbs 18:21)

It has rightfully been said that words matter and, often times, words can have deadly consequences. "In the beginning was the Word, and the Word was with God, and the Word was God. The same was in the beginning with God. All things were made by him; and without him was not anything made that was made" (John 1:1-2). Moreover, "A soft answer turneth away wrath: but grievous words stir up anger" (Proverbs 15:1). In fact, ungodly words incite devilish actions; however, "The words of the Lord are pure words: as silver tried in a furnace of earth, purified seven times" (Psalms 12:6). However, there is a thin line between ungodly words and evil actions.

To be sure, everyone that says, "Lord, Lord," does not necessarily mean it. Since words matter, individuals should be very careful regarding the words they utter to each other. This is precisely why the Bible declares: "Let the words of my mouth, and the meditation of my heart (mind), be acceptable in thy sight, O Lord, my strength, and my redeemer" (Psalm 19:14). More importantly, every American should understand: "For as he thinketh in his heart, so is he: Eat and drink, saith he to thee; but his heart is not with thee" (Proverbs 23:7). Therefore, "Walk in wisdom toward them that are without, redeeming the time. Let your speech be always with grace, seasoned with salt, that ye may know how ye ought to answer every man" (Colossians 4:5-6). Hence, on both sides of the political equation, when we operate out of written scriptural words, we are on the Lord's side; we can all walk together, and we, most assuredly, give no place to the devil. For after all, "Can two walk together, except they be agreed?" (Amos 3:3). America, be mindful and ever so careful because we only have one choice between God and the devil. Hence, the real choices are spiritual choices, not the political choices of Democratic versus Republican.

And, just in case you have conveniently developed amnesia or malnutrition of the brain, please be reminded that the choice has already been established, stated, and emphatically declared with the precious blood already shed: "That we hold these truths to be self-evident...," in America's Preamble to the Constitution and the Articles of the U.S. Constitution. After all, "There is no wisdom nor understanding nor counsel against the Lord" (Proverbs 23:7). The U.S. Constitution is a spiritual document written primarily by God-fearing men. Therefore, the Constitution matters. Question: Which do Americans love more—the Constitution or partisan politics?

As Americans, we all know "righteousness exalteth a nation: but sin is a reproach to any people" (Proverbs 14:34). And, through God's word, we should all know that "the house of the wicked shall be overthrown: but the tabernacle of the upright shall flourish" (Proverbs 14:11). As men and women of God, let's embrace the will of God, and above all, the teachings of our Lord and Savior Jesus Christ, the Righteous One, because "we must all appear before the judgment seat of Christ; that every one may receive the things done in his body, according to that which he hath done, whether it be good or bad" (2 Corinthians 5:10). Without a doubt, "Every one of us shall give in account of himself to God" (Romans 14:12). Therefore, through these scriptural "spiritual" precepts we should "be not deceived: evil communications corrupts good manners. Awake to righteousness, and sin not, for some have not the knowledge of God: I speak this to your shame" (1 Corinthians 15:33-34). We should always remember that no individual can hide from the Word of God. Therefore, "Be not deceived; God is not mocked: for whatsoever a man soweth, that shall he also reap. For he that soweth to his flesh shall of the flesh reap corruption; but he that soweth to the Spirit shall of the Spirit reap life everlasting. And let us not be weary in well doing: for in due season we shall reap, if we faint not. As we have therefore opportunity; let us do good unto all men, especially unto them who are of the household of faith" (Galatians 6:7-10).

America's spiritual and political leadership problem is grounded in the inability of Christian pastoral leaders to foster a spiritual-focused moral ought. In fact, in Christendom, we have too many pastoral sell-outs: "His watchmen are blind: they are ignorant, they are all dumb dogs, they cannot bark; sleeping, lying down, loving to slumber" (Isaiah 56:10). Primarily pastoral leaders are teaching and preaching what church goers want to hear, and not what they need to spiritually know. There is a spiritual heaven and hell. Make no mistake about it. Therefore, the worst place for your soul to ever reside eternally is in a spiritual hell, especially after having lived in a physical hell on earth. Hence, pastoral leaders embrace, in totality, the unadulterated word of God because "the word of God is quick, and powerful, and sharper than any two-edged sword" (Hebrews 4:12). It is written, "Let us therefore come boldly unto the throne of grace, that we may obtain mercy, and find grace to help in time of need" (Hebrews 4:16).

For it is as certain as the sun rising in the East and setting in the West: "As it is appointed unto men once to die, but after this the judgment: so Christ was once offered to bear the sins of many; and unto them that look for him shall he appear the second time without sin unto salvation" (Hebrews 9:27-28). God is the judge, and "God judgeth the righteous, and God is angry with the wicked every day" (Psalm 7:11). Hear well, pastoral leaders: foretold is forewarned. "The heads thereof judge for reward, and the priests thereof teach for hire, and the prophets thereof divine for money: yet will they lean upon the Lord, and say, Is not the Lord among us? none evil can come upon us" (Micah 3:11).

Christians all over the world, "Be sober, be vigilant; because your adversary the devil, as a roaring lion, walketh about, seeking whom he may devour: whom resist stedfast in the faith, knowing that the same afflictions are accomplished in your brethren that are in the world" (1 Peter 5:8-9). Pastoral leaders, God's desire is that you shepherd his people toward righteousness for Christ's sake. Therefore, "Submit yourselves to God. Resist the devil, and he will flee from you." (James 4:7). Selah!

Politics In The Best Interest Of Democracy

2015 marks the fiftieth anniversary of the passage of the 1965 Voting Rights Act. Voting is a constitutional right that should never be taken for granted. Let's not just enjoy the theme song Glory in the historic movie about Selma, but let's be a participant in voting our conscience for the glory of God. Vote your conscience and in the morning you shall see the glory of God. Blood was shed and precious lives lost in order that all Americans have the sacred privilege of voting. Shame, shame, and more shame on those Americans who fail to exercise the constitutional privilege of voting in every election. All politics is local; therefore, vote for those candidates that best represent the interests of America. Minorities and fair-minded Whites understand the injustice of some who are hell bent on preventing minorities from exercising their Constitutional right to vote.

The scripture below clearly identifies the nature of the spiritual, moral, and political problems that are plaguing America: "For men shall be lovers of their own selves, covetous, boasters, proud, blasphemers, disobedient to parents, unthankful, unholy, without natural affection, trucebreakers, false accusers, incontinent, fierce, despisers of those that are good, traitors, heady, high-minded, lovers of pleasure more than lovers of God; having a form of godliness, but denying the power thereof: from such turn away. For of this sort are they which creep into houses, and lead captive silly women laden with sins, led away with divers lusts, ever learning, and never able to come to the knowledge of the truth" (2 Timothy 3:2-8). In the past, Blacks who were free to vote voted for Republicans because of President Abraham Lincoln (Emancipation Proclamation). Many Whites also voted Republican. The Democratic Party (Dixiecrats) historically was the party of slavery, and the Republican Party was the party of freedom. But, oh how Southern Dixiecrats have jumped ship in the South once again seeking to protect White privilege. The more things change the more they remain the same.

Blacks vote Democratic primarily because of a perceived "big tent" political philosophy that includes rather than excludes. The Republican Party's political approach to governing perceptually undergirds the notion of "White Privilege". This is primarily why the Republican Party is ninety-two percent White, and the Democratic Party is over sixty-five percent minority. Pitting one racial/ethnic group against another racial/ethnic groups is not a healthy formula for a harmonious, democratic America. The battle-cry of the present-day Republican Party is Reaganomics—trickle-down-economics. Their philosophical slogan is, "let's take our country back." Question: Take the country back from whom and for what purpose? When did Whites lose socio-economic-political control over America? Whites still own 90% of all economic assets even though America is browning. Both political party approaches to democratic governance are about power-politics, and what is perceived to be in their political party's best interests. Achieving power sharing among diverse racial and ethnic groups in a multi-cultural society is a complicated political process. On the one hand, at one time, what was the old Southern-Dixiecrat

Party is now the twenty-first century Republican Party. Southern Dixiecrats (southern states) blamed the slaves, not the Union, for their demise during the Civil War. Slaves had no power but to do or die. Even in the year 2015 it seems that way. Questions: What happened to the party of Lincoln? How did the party of Lincoln become the party of perceived White Privilege with a Dixiecrat twist? Seemingly, the objective is to find ways to exclude minorities from the electoral process at any cost. But, more importantly, this attitudinal political initiative excludes minorities from achieving the American Dream. And, at the same time, they blame the victim for everything that is wrong with America (e.g., Welfare).

Poor Whites are political pawns caught in the middle of something that is beyond their intellectual comprehension because of institutional racism. That is, poor Whites as well as some middle class Whites are not politically sophisticated enough to understand the strategy of divide-and-conquer. If they do, they turn a blind eye to the real cause of their own socio-economic plight. This set of circumstances tends to trivialize the economic contributions of Blacks to the economic success of America as slaves and second-class citizens (Jim-Crowism). In the twenty-first century, after almost 400 years, Blacks are still on the outside of the socio-economic mainstream looking-in. These facts account for why Blacks remain a separate socio-economic class. However, Blacks must continue to fight the good fight, keep the faith, and God will give the faithful a crown of righteousness.

How do we achieve a just democratic society? The answer lies in spiritual (biblical truths) and moral obedience, because obedience is greater than sacrifice—especially when individuals are seeking truth, wisdom, and spiritual understanding. Democracy is for a spiritually enlightened citizenry. "Study to show thyself approved unto God, a workman that needeth not to be ashamed, rightly dividing the word of truth" (2 Timothy 2:15). Obedience is the only foundation for self-development as well as a healthy democratic society. Let's clearly understand what is currently operating in America in our two-party political system;,which in turn, is causing untold political and moral governing confusion—especially in one particular political party (Republican Party). While, on the other hand, the Democratic Party is killing America softly attempting to make sin an issue of civil rights. God is God. Civil rights are not God.

There is a clarion-call blowing in the wind in America: Change direction before it is too late, and God pulls down the curtain, and the sun sets on America. Americans must learn anew how to please God and love and serve each other. The unadulterated disrespect of both the office of the presidency, as well as the man, began with the election of President Barack Obama. When Americans come to themselves, and know the one true God and Jesus Christ whom He has sent, this insanity will be a thing of the past. Selah!

WHERE DO WE GO FROM HERE: COMMUNITY OR CHAOS?

During the Civil Rights Movement of the 1960's, Dr. Martin Luther King, Jr. asked this profound spiritual question: Where do we go from here: community or chaos? And since that time, America has steadily been marching toward national chaos rather than national unity. And, of course, the 2016 presidential election brought the under-current of racial discord to an apex. Question: What is the cultural plan of black people other than the instinct to survive to stay here another day? We know God's spiritual plan, but what is the cultural plan of action for insisting that America live up to the spiritual meaning of its solemn creed: "We hold these Truths to be self-evident, that all Men are created equal, that they are endowed by their Creator with certain unalienable Rights, that among these are Life, Liberty, and the Pursuit of Happiness."

Jesus has already died for our sins; therefore, we do not have to die again, but learn how to creatively live. But, a Christian must be willing to die for the sake of righteousness, because "righteousness exalteth a nation: but sin is a reproach to any people." (Proverbs 14: 34). Our plan of action as Christians is to build the Kingdom of God on earth as it is in Heaven. There is nothing difficult about this, because there is nothing too hard for God. As Christians, in order to help individuals transcend the color line spiritually and intellectually, we must be willing to die for the sake of righteous principles and godly teaching in order to live for a righteous cause.

Dr. King said it best in the letter from the Birmingham Jail in which he writes about the higher morality and spirituality of self-purification. Injustice should not be tolerated in American society. And those who are the victims of societal injustice should self-purify in order to not participate in their own self-victimization. Words without deeds are the epitome of immorality. Saying one thing and doing another is not self-purification, but self-denigration. Of course, saying, "Lord, Lord," and running with the devil is a sin. The letter from the Birmingham Jail ought to be canonized in the black Christian experience and be displayed in every black church in America.

In the shadow of deep disappointment regarding the race based policies of discrimination in Birmingham, Alabama, at that time, Dr. King wrote about taking direct action in the struggle for basic Civil Rights: "We had no alternative except to prepare for direct action, whereby we would present our bodies as a means of laying our case before the conscience of the local and national community. Mindful of the difficulties involved, we decided to undertake a process of self-purification. We began a series of workshops on nonviolence, and we repeatedly asked ourselves: Are you able to accept blows without retaliating? Are you able to endure the ordeal of jail?" *(Letter From the Birmingham Jail, MLK Research and Education Institute)*.

The spirituality of the Civil Rights Movement is laid bare in MLK's letter from the Birmingham jail. Remember now, there were many black pastoral leaders that were highly critical of Dr. King. The black church, especially in the South, was the hub for the Civil Rights movement. And, black pastoral leaders were dedicated spiritual men providing guidance for business development, educational development and civic quality of life, and family relationships. Black power and black pride were more than just mere emotional slogans, but these slogans were attitudes and social behaviors that were transformed into life styles.

If the black community is to thrive spiritually, economically, and educationally, black pastors must rekindle this developmental spirit in the black church community. Before black people can hold the purveyors of socio-economic injustices (whites) accountable, they must first engage themselves in a process of self-examination, and if need be, self-purification. This is precisely why associate editor, Jeffrey L. Boney, asked the question: "Where in the hell is the black church?"

To be sure, the 2016 presidential election has ushered in spiritual warfare to the nth degree, and above all, absolute moral confusion. This is a statement of fact; ultimately, every individual is accountable for his or her own actions. Therefore, sin is not a Civil Rights issue, but a God issue. The failure, especially of black religious leaders, to boldly speak out against those who are violating gospel singer Kim Burrell's civil rights is a sinful disgrace before God. Ms. Burrell simply made a godly statement of spiritual truth because she has studied this Biblical truth: "Study to shew thyself approved unto God, a workman that needeth not to be ashamed, rightly dividing the word of truth" (2 Timothy 2:15). God gave every individual free will. If we choose to sin against God and doubt God's word, then it is between the individual and God. Because, "God judgeth the righteous, and God is angry with the wicked every day" (Psalm 7:11). As Christians, we must remember to: "Lay hands suddenly on no man, neither be partaker of other men's sins: keep thyself pure" (1 Timothy 5:22). Unfortunately, we are not becoming better people but bitter people because of America's religious, political, and educational leadership. The model for leadership is Jesus Christ.

Again, as Dr. King asked: "Where do we go from here?" Let's pray that it is not to hell in a hand-basket. God does not need everybody, He just needs somebody: ask Gideon, ask King David, ask Joshua, ask Nathan, ask Abraham Lincoln, ask Lyndon Johnson, ask Dr. M. L. King, Jr., ask Mary McLeod Bethune, ask Madame C.J. Walker, ask Eleanor Roosevelt, ask Michelle Obama, ask Barack Obama. But, most of all, let's ask Jesus Christ the Righteous One: "But grow in grace, and in the knowledge of our Lord and Savior Jesus Christ. To him be glory both now and forever" (2 Peter 3:18).

As Christians, pastors and laity, we must, at this time, pray for righteous judgment against evil-doers, and be prepared as was Dr. King to fight the good spiritual fight for justice for all as Gideon had to fight. Then, we all can boldly declare, "Free at last, free at-last, thank God almighty, we're free at last." Selah!

VANITY

All Christians know that the wisest and richest man to have ever lived was compelled to declare, "Vanity of vanities; all is vanity" (Ecclesiastes 1:2). In all of King Solomon's glory he could not escape from this revelatory knowledge of God: "There is no wisdom nor understanding nor counsel against the Lord" (Proverbs 21:30). Solomon, just like many of us, became enthralled in his own lustful desires. God warned him about "messing with strange fruit." It's a profound spiritual truth—"don't mess with them apples"—because the apple of a man's eye is and will always be a woman, not another man. Of course, there is a profound difference between man and male. Man is about spirituality and male is about biology (nature).

More importantly, faithful Christians know that "the fear of the Lord is the instruction of wisdom; and before honor is humility" (Proverbs 15:33). King Solomon feared God, and this is precisely why he asked God for wisdom that he might be able to lead people in the "path of the Lord" (righteousness). King Solomon learned this spiritual lesson the hard way: "Before destruction the heart of man is haughty; and before honor is humility" (Proverbs 18:12). When all is said and done, King Solomon went for the okey-doke. That is, he "messed" with strange women, and strange women do not know God, and above all, they worship idols. Many individuals believe, and of course there is some truth in the phrase: "Good girls go to heaven, but bad girls go everywhere." Maybe King Solomon thought that he could change the paradigm. But, my fellow Americans, when God gives a "spiritual warning," obey the spiritual warning; if you do not, disaster is waiting around the corner. God warned King Solomon personally. God is warning America through his written word: "And even as they did not like to retain God in their knowledge, God gave them over to a reprobate mind, to do those things which are not convenient; being filled with all unrighteousness…" (Romans 1:28-32).

God has forewarned all individuals: "For the invisible things of Him from the creation of the world are clearly seen, being understood by the things that are made, even his eternal power and God-head; so that they are without excuse…" (Romans 1:20). Even Caesar (mankind) had enough "common-sense" knowledge to go to the Bible and state emphatically: "ignorance of the law is no excuse." "Blessed is he that readeth, and they that hear the words of this prophecy, and keep those things which are written therein: for the time is at hand" (Revelations 1:3).

Solomon asked God for wisdom, but God gave Solomon both wisdom and enormous riches beyond his wildest imagination. Additionally, he inherited the throne of Israel from his father King David, and more importantly, God anointed him in the position because he asked God for wisdom rather than riches.

Some individuals do not know when they have the spiritual victory, because they think they deserve it and others do not, because personal vanity against God consumes them. I sincerely believe that both King David and King Solomon knew that they were blessed. But, unfortunately, both neglected to hide the Word of God in the heart of their minds in order that they might not sin against God. "Thy word have I hid in mine heart, that I might not sin against thee" (Psalm 119:11). King David had a Hittite warrior killed (Uriah) in order to cover up his sin with Uriah's wife (Bathsheba). King Solomon, David's son, was the offspring of the marital union between King David and Bathsheba. Of course, King Solomon consorted with strange women against God's admonishment not to have personal dealings with strange women. Strange women believe in the vanity of the idol gods of this world: gold, silver, jewelry, cars, and fine clothes.

On the other hand, Enoch was the son of Cain, an individual that killed his own brother, and lied to God about the killing, declaring, "Am I my brother's keeper?" The Bible states that Enoch walked with God, that is, he ordered his thoughts and behavior by God's word. All individuals should order their steps by the word of God. And, for Enoch's faithfulness, the Bible states: "And Enoch walked with God; and he was not, for God took him" (Genesis 5:24). That is, Enoch was raptured into the joy of the Lord. "Can two walk together, except they are agreed?" (Amos 3:3).

We are living in spiritually perilous and morally decadent times whereby humankind is spiritually waxing cold. Spiritual and moral decadence is worse than Ebola, because moral decadence eats away at the soul of individuals, as well as the soul of a nation-state. The Ebola virus only eats away at the flesh (body), because Ebola is caused by uncleanliness of body and physical environment. In fact, America is in a state of spiritual and moral confusion whereby too many individuals are hell-bent on taking wrong, and making it right, and making it work for a short while. The end does not necessarily justify the means.

Vanity has led too many Americans into the wilderness of being devoid of moral character. "And because iniquity shall abound, the love of many shall wax cold. But he that shall endure unto the end, the same shall be saved" (Matthew 24:12-13). But, "This know also, that in the last days perilous times shall come. For men shall be lovers of their own selves, covetous, boasters, proud, blasphemers, disobedient to parents, unthankful, unholy, without natural affection, trucebreakers, false accusers, incontinent, fierce, despisers of those that are good, traitors, heady, high-minded, lovers of pleasures more than lovers of God; having a form of godliness, but denying the power thereof; from such turn away" (2 Timothy 3:1-6).

Without a doubt, vanity prevents individuals from ever coming to the truth about the meaning of life and relationships. We have come full circle in American society: "For the time will come when they will not endure sound doctrine; but after their own lusts shall they heap to themselves teachers, having itching ears; and they shall turn away their ears from the truth, and shall be turned unto fables" (2 Timothy 4:3-4).

Politicians promise citizens liberty, and at the same time, make them servants of socio-economic corruption. Statesmen serve the best interests of the nation as well as that of the next generation. More importantly, we have some pastoral leaders peddling (preaching) material prosperity while spiritually enslaving parishioners to the vulgar, materialistic building of their own personal kingdoms rather than the Kingdom of God.

Question: Who can deliver us from the spiritual corruption of this world? The answer is God, God, and only God. In conclusion, King Solomon, with all of his godly wisdom and enormous wealth, had to testify that all is vanity, vanity. In essence this is what King Solomon was saying: "For what shall it profit a man, if he shall gain the whole world, and lose his own soul?" (Mark 8:37). Amen.

AMERICA NEEDS PRAYERFUL/SPIRITUAL LEADERSHIP

Social democracy demands an educated and spiritually well-informed citizenry. The Bible states, "Blessed is he that readeth, and they that hear the words of this prophecy, and keep those things which are written therein: for the time is at hand" (Revelation 1:3). This is precisely why the Founders were most creative in their desire to educate the masses in order to achieve a "more perfect union," and therefore, they created a mass universal public educational system.

The soul of America is held captive by vulgar secularism, an insatiable greed for money as the ultimate source of power, and the grand mis-guided notion of white privilege. Christians worship God (Creator); not things (creation). By the way, America, in case you did not know it, money is not God.

Individuals can run, but they cannot hide from God and divine judgment, because: "Every house is builded by some man; but he that built all things is God" (Hebrews 3:4). But, more importantly, "Thou art worthy, O Lord, to receive glory and honor and power: for thou hast created all things, and for thy pleasure they are and were created" (Revelation 4:11).

America has created a powder-keg of vulgar secularism, spiritual and moral confusion, rather than godly understanding about the nature of social democracy. To be sure, social democracy requires an intelligent and informed voting population. This is why strong-man dictatorships only exist in Third World underdeveloped nations. Indeed, it is unfortunate that twenty-first century America has too many ill-educated and uninformed but eligible voters (citizens). This and only this can explain the rise of a dictatorial leadership style like that of a Donald Trump in American society.

Make America Great Again is a radical ungodly appeal to the emotional insecurity that some Whites feel concerning power and political control. Substituting emotional insecurity and intensity for wisdom, spiritual understanding, and knowledge is a political recipe for national disaster. However, this is a manmade, socio-political-economic equation without godly understanding, because it is too easy to forget: "There is no wisdom nor understanding nor counsel against the Lord" (Proverbs 21:30). Therefore, every human being should remember this profound scripture: "Man that is born of woman is of a few days, and full of trouble. He cometh forth like a flower, and is cut down: he fleeth also as a shadow, and continueth not" (Job 14:1-2). Neither money, nor any other earthly thing can provide immortality to individuals, because "it is appointed unto men once to die, but after this the judgment" (Hebrews 9:27). And, without a doubt: "God judgeth the righteous, and God is angry with the wicked every day" (Hebrews 7:11).

America needs spiritual, thoughtful, mature, and moral leadership that is oriented toward the the U.S. Declaration of Independence, which says, "We hold these truths to be self-evident, that all men are created equal, that they are endowed by their Creator with certain unalienable Rights, that among these are Life, Liberty and the pursuit of Happiness; That to secure these rights, Governments are instituted among Men, deriving their just powers from the consent of the governed."

American political leaders are attempting to deal with daily, life and death decision-making based upon carnal-minded misunderstanding. Scripture warns us concerning this type of secularized leadership mentality: "Trust in the Lord with all thine heart; and lean not unto thine own understanding. In all thine ways acknowledge him, and he shall direct thy paths. Be not wise in thine own eyes: fear the Lord and depart from evil (idolatry, inordinate affection, same-sex marriage, idol gods, and so on)" (Proverbs 3:5-7). Because, we all know, that: "The steps of a good man are ordered by the Lord, and he delighteth in his way" (Psalms 37:23). Therefore, at all times, Americans should "let all things be done decently and in order" (1 Corinthians 14:40).

In the twenty first century, too many individuals are exposing their private sexual lives publicly. Too many men want to be women—the vanity-oriented feminization of American culture. And, vice versa, too many women want to be men. Thus, America's children are confused concerning what to become. But, most of all, too few want to be what God created them to be: Children of God. It is indeed an unfortunate set of circumstances that too many Americans have become vanity-oriented, possessing an uncontrollable and ungodly desire for things. Vulgar secularism and moral confusion are common place.

Seemingly, there is no political-leadership solution(s) to the horrible societal mess we find ourselves in. But, hold on for a minute, and don't despair; there is an answer in JESUS.

America has more guns than citizens. But are we safe from ourselves? We kill and steal from each other in time, on time, all the time, and for no godly reason. However, the murder rate is declining; not because of more guns in the hands of citizens, but because of spiritual conscience and moral values. We must do a better job in our family environments and churches of socio-economically educating and socializing our children toward civilized, moral conduct. Killing for pleasure and things is evil and wicked.

America, "Be sober, be vigilant; because your adversary the devil, as a roaring lion, walketh about, seeking whom he may devour..." (1 Peter 5:8-9). But, more importantly, my fellow Americans: "Submit yourselves therefore to God. Resist the devil, and he will flee from you. Draw nigh to God, and he will draw nigh to you... Speak not evil one of another, brethren..." (James 4:7-12). Selah!

Day Versus Night: Light Versus Dark

The difference between what once was and what currently is is the difference between day and night and light and dark. America currently has a President that bears witness to this spiritual fact. "I and I alone can fix it." America, believe me, this is truly the "I" that is smack-dab in the middle of sin. God is the only self-sufficient "I." Therefore, "Blessed is the man that walketh not in the counsel of the ungodly, nor standeth in the way of sinners, nor sitteth in the seat of the scornful. But his delight is in the law of the Lord; and in his law doth he meditate day and night" (Psalm 1:1-2). Black men, beware; in fact, be careful whose side you are on. The reason being: He "who his own self bare our sins in his own body on the tree, that we, being dead to sins, should live unto righteousness: by whose stripes ye were healed. For ye were as sheep going astray; but are now returned unto the Shepherd and Bishop of your souls" (1 Peter 2:24-25). We know that there are a few Black men who are seemingly not on the Lord's side, but are on President Trump's side. Therefore, we must be sober, and vigilant in watching them, but most of all pray for them. Beware of the hypocrisy of darkness: "Therefore whatsoever ye have spoken in darkness shall be heard in the light; and that which ye have spoken in the ear in closets shall be proclaimed upon the housetops" (Luke 12:3).

When we were in the Garden of Eden, God warned us not to eat of the Tree of the Knowledge of Good and Evil in the center of the Garden, but we could eat of all others. And, we all know the consequences: SIN. Disobedience to God was the first sin. Lying about sin compounded the original sin. Likewise, President Trump forewarned America and the world community concerning who he really is. In fact, he told us that he has a dictatorial mind, but neglected to tell us about his sexist, masochistic, racist, and money-oriented mind. More importantly, he showed America that he has a lying tongue. How do you know when President Trump is lying? When his lips are moving.

The Russians are not coming. The Russian mentality has been in America for a long time. And, on January 20th, 2017 the Russian mentality (dictatorship) invaded the White House, the world's symbol of social democracy, human rights, leadership of the free world, and freedom of individual choice. Life is about choices and consequences. President Trump is never introspective, and always blames others, especially the "fake news media." President Trump says that he has inherited a "mess", and at the time, he is creating a monumental mess at home and abroad. We have always had problems with Russia (Cuban Missile Crisis), North Korea, Iran (hostage crisis), the Middle East (Jews-Palestinians), and so on. However, the problems are being compounded by the ineptness of Trump's administrative style.

Americans should absolutely be ashamed of themselves for exposing the world community to a mentality such as Donald J. Trump's— especially with all of this nation's talented young men and women. Shamefully, forty-eight percent of the American voting populace voted for Donald J. Trump as the 45th President. President Trump represents the symbol of leadership not only in America, but also the "free world." Donald J. Trump is the President of these United States of America, but it does not mean that he is the right moral leader for these United States of America. "For God is not the author of confusion, but of peace, as in all churches of the saints" (1 Corinthians 14:34). We have compounded confusion in the White House. Moreover, President Trump is destroying the basic democratic institutional fabric of American society while the Russians and the devil laugh at our spiritual and moral stupidity.

Again, allow me to reiterate: the 2016 presidential election was not about jobs, trade agreements, or the repealing of the Affordable Healthcare Act (so-called Obamacare), but white privilege. In fact, the primary subliminal reason why the Affordable Healthcare Act is called Obamacare is because of the skin color of the president. President Obama was viewed by some as an illegitimate president simply because of his skin color. The Republican Party leadership declared publicly that the objective was "to make Obama a one-term President," and above all, not to agree with any proposed legislative initiatives of the Obama Administration. Republicans legislators put party loyalty before country. Every Presidential action taken by Obama was deemed illegitimate and dead on arrival. Institutional racism is spiritually grounded in the irrationality (emotional rhetoric) of the devil's lies, not the reality and rationality of God. Moreover, for far too long, the Republican Party has been attempting to disguise tenets of institutional racism under the mantle and rubric of conservatism. Now, the presidency of Donald J. Trump has bit Republicans, as well as American society in the preverbial behind. But, more importantly, it has revealed the nature of our very existence as a democratic society that is oriented toward white privilege. Republicans, take a moral stand. Demand to see President Trump's tax returns.

At one time, white high school graduates were earning more than some public school teachers, and even some college professors. Multinational corporations are primarily concerned with bottom-line economics, and therefore, they shipped high-paying working class jobs overseas for cheap labor and corporate profits. Now, white working class individuals seeking additional skills and technical training, stop crying, moaning, and groaning, get up off your behinds, acquire more formal education for high-tech (meaningful wage) jobs, and you will be able to obtain a high-tech job and experience the American Dream, and not simply because you are white. For after all, minorities—especially blacks—are the last hired and the first fired.

Of course, gaining a formal education just might awaken your spiritual thinking ability about presidential leadership, and more importantly, what to vote for, because money is not the answer. Leadership is about moral character and intellectual integrity. What is inscribed on the money is the ultimate answer: "In God We Trust." But, more importantly, God sent Jesus Christ as the living example, because "Jesus Christ is the same yesterday, and today, and forever" (Hebrews 13:8). More importantly, "A little that a righteous man hath is better than the riches of many wicked" (Psalm 37:16).

Lying Does Not Alter Reality

There is no such thing as an alternative reality based upon alternative facts. The Bible teaches us clearly what alternative facts are: "profane and vain babblings: for they will increase unto more ungodliness" (2 Timothy 2:16). There is only truth based upon God' reality, not individual and institutional LYING, because equal is equal, not more or less equal. In our Christian churches, we know this spiritual TRUTH, but we cannot live the reality of this eternal truth. "Woe unto you, scribes and Pharisees, Hypocrites! For ye pay tithe of mint and anise and cumin, and have omitted the weightier matters of the law, judgment, mercy, and faith: these ye ought to have done, and not leave the other undone. Ye blind guides, which strain at a gnat, and swallow a camel" (Matthew 23:23-24).

Foretold is forewarned. Moreover, ultimate reality is reality as God intended it to be because "The earth is the Lord's, and the fullness thereof; the world, and they that dwell therein" (Psalms 24:1). The irreverent lying of Trump Administration officials is leading America into a state of utter moral chaos and spiritual confusion, and will ultimately end in war. If individuals continue to play with fire, eventually they will be burned, and their children will be burned as well. "Six things doth the Lord hate: yea, seven are an abomination unto him: A proud look, a lying tongue, and hands that shed innocent blood" (Proverbs 6:16-17). The Question of Questions is: Can anything good come out of Trump Tower via The White House? It does not appear to be so given what we have seen and heard since January 20th, 2017. Because lies operate off of borrowed energy, and the truth creates its own energy that stands alone.

The White House has been transformed into The House of Lies. Systemic serial lying by Trump officials has produced the Rule of Trump, not the Rule of Law based upon democratic tenets. Democracy is built upon the rule of LAW, and above all, truth telling. President Trump's moral approach to governance is based upon a businessman's agenda which includes the few, and excludes the many. Democracy is of the people, by the people, and for the people. The Trump Administration agenda is not a citizen agenda. This is why President Trump views trade as a zero sum game rather than a mutual benefit game. Moreover, Trump officials do not understand that if individuals tell the truth they do not have to remember (recall) what they said. And, here's the long and short of it: "For the law of the Spirit of life in Christ Jesus hath made me free from the law of sin and death" (Romans 8:2). Trump Administration Officials: Stop Lying. Because, we all should know and know without a doubt that: "Righteousness exalteth a nation: but sin is a reproach to any people" (Proverbs 14:34). Moreover, lying is the beginning of Sin, and individuals should not bear false witness against one another. Shame! Shame! Shame on you, President Trump for lying for General Flynn, and lying on former FBI Director Comey. Christian Evangelicals, since you voted for President Trump please inform him that "There is no wisdom nor understanding nor counsel against the Lord" (Proverbs 21:30).

America, pray for the Trump Administration: "If my people, which are called by my name, shall humble themselves, and pray, and seek my face, and turn from their wicked ways; then will I hear from heaven, and will forgive their sin, and will heal their land." (2 Chronicles 7: 14).

Seemingly, the approach to democratic governance by Trump Officials is based upon lower class value constructs (gutter rats) rather than middle class democratic values. America has entered into an era of government by personality rather than democratic institutional policies and procedures which, in turn, are grounded in time honored democratic tenets. The integrity of America's democratic institutions and "political" system of governance is slowly drifting into ungodly partisan politics. And, by the way, this is why so many Americans commonly believe that politics is a pile of manure, and consequently do not participate in the political (electoral) process (voting).

Alternative facts ultimately entice individuals into sinning against God, self, and country. Above all, this is precisely why individuals must always remember that: "A wise man feareth, and departed from evil: but the fool rageth, and is confident" (Proverbs 14:16). Jesus is physically gone, but it's not goodbye, because some of us shall be caught-up in the blinking of an eye in the sky with our Lord and Savior Jesus Christ. Therefore, all Americans must clearly understand that alternative facts are grounded in lying, and therefore, we must spiritually guard ourselves against carnal mindedness and resist the unreality of alternative facts: "For to be carnally minded is death; but to be spiritually minded is life and peace. Because the carnal mind is enmity against God: for it is not subject to the law of God, neither indeed can be. So then they that are in the flesh cannot please God" (Romans 8:6-8).

The rule of law is the spiritual cornerstone principle of social democracy. For after all, it is "Obedience" to law which invariably preserves the integrity of democratic governmental institutions: Government of laws versus government of men. Moreover, my fellow Americans, God is not mocked nor is He fooled, individuals reap what they sow. Therefore, understand: "Nevertheless the foundation of God standeth sure, having this seal, The Lord knoweth them that are his. And, Let everyone that nameth the name of Christ depart from iniquity (SIN)" (2 Timothy 2:19).

Republicans, this is not a sermonette, but a spiritual reminder of the power of The Word of God. Therefore, understand and embrace this spiritual truism: "There is a way which seemeth right unto a man, but the end thereof are the ways of death" (Proverbs 14:12). The Republican Party is being victimized by ungodly group think and hijacked by White Privilege-oriented nationalism. The spirit of Abraham Lincoln is probably aggrieved at the pathetic desire of most Republicans for power, privilege, and money without collective responsibility for the well-being of the greatest democratic nation on the planet. Just a spiritual reminder: "The house of the wicked shall be overthrown: but the tabernacle of the upright shall flourish" (Proverbs 14:11). The world is watching in utter dismay at what is being said and done by the Trump Administration, but more importantly, God has pure eyes, He sees and hears everything at the same time. "Thou art of purer eyes than to behold evil, and canst not look on iniquity, wherefore lookest thou upon them that deal treacherously, and holdest thy tongue when the wicked devoureth the man that is more righteous than he?" (Habakkuk 1: 13). The bad joke in The White House has become America's horrible nightmare on 1600 Pennsylvania Avenue. Selah!

WHAT SEPARATES AMERICANS FROM EACH OTHER?

President Abraham Lincoln said it best: "A house (nation) divided against itself cannot stand." More importantly, what separates Americans from each other is SIN, and sin engenders separation from God. Above all, separation from God is separation from ultimate reality, because God is reality. "The earth is the Lord's, and the fullness thereof, the world and they that dwell therein. For he hath founded it upon the seas, and established it upon the floods" (Psalm 24:1-2). If God had not so loved the world, and sent his only begotten Son, Jesus Christ, to save the world from sin, then individuals would have an excuse for sin. "Christ also suffered for us, leaving us an example, that ye should follow his steps: who did no sin, neither was guile found in his mouth: who, when he was reviled, reviled not again; when he suffered, he threatened not; but committed himself to him that judgeth righteously: who his own self bare our sins in his own body on the tree, that we, being dead to sins, should live unto righteousness: by whose stripes ye were healed" (1 Peter 2:21-24). America has a real God problem because too many Americans are separated from the reality of God.

We are separated from the spiritual reality of God, and this is why we are divided as a nation-state. Too many Americans are in conflict with self (SELF is the enemy and GOD is the solution). A problem with self invariably leads to having problems with others. Self-hatred engenders hatred toward others. In fact, God is the solution to the pollution and minutiae that is in the heart of our minds as well as the environment. But, God has the last word. Confusion is of the devil and peace is of God. "For God is not the author of confusion, but of peace, as in all churches of the saints" (1 Corinthians 14:33). To be sure, what has historically divided us is skin color, even though God created all of us in his image, a little lower than angels. For after all, if any individual has a problem with the skin color of another individual, take it up with God. Once again, God made us all. Moreover, righteous judgment belongs to God, because "There is a way which seemeth right unto a man, but the end thereof are the ways of death" (Proverbs 14:12). But, more importantly, "It is written, As I live, saith the Lord, every knee shall bow to me, and every tongue shall confess to God. So then every one of us shall give account of himself to God. Let us not therefore judge one another anymore: but judge this rather, that no man put a stumbling block or an occasion to fail in his brother's way" (Romans 14:12-13). America, it is written: "But many that are first shall be last; and the last shall be first" (Matthew 19:30). Be careful, America, God still sits on the throne, and He is watching you: "God judgeth the righteous, and God is angry with the wicked" (Psalm 7:11).

God has asked every individual as well as every nation-state before undertaking making money or building earthly kingdoms: "But seek ye first the kingdom of God, and his righteousness; and all these other things shall be added unto you" (Matthew 6:33). God desires this for only one reason: In order that individuals might be prepared to handle the vanity of the world, because when an individual follows after vanity, he/she is void of understanding. "The man that wandereth out of the way of understanding shall remain in the congregation (nation) of the dead" (Proverbs 21:16). Therefore, do not become a card-carrying member of the walking dead club. America, this too shall pass away.

God hates racism, and racism is a sin against God's will. Indeed, God clearly desires that all individuals understand this verse: "Thy word have I hid in mine heart, that I might not sin against thee" (Psalm 119:11).

Now, we come to the heart of the matter: What is it that can unite Americans as one nation under God, indivisible with liberty and justice for all? That is the question of questions? And, the answer is GOD.

The first order of godly business is the spiritual revitalization of the family unit in American society. Society begins in the nuclear family unit, and God is the designer of the family, not the U.S. Supreme Court. Any law against GOD is a bad law. God asked Job: "Where were you when I laid the foundation of the earth?" (Job 38:4). A similar question can be asked of the U.S. Supreme Court. "Where were you when God created Adam and Eve (not Adam and Steve or Eve and Evelyn)? God gave Adam and Eve a four-fold foundation for godly living: "Be fruitful, and multiply, and replenish the earth, and have dominion over..." (Genesis 1:27-28). There are some things that should not be legislated because God gave us free will to make choices. And individuals must live and die by the choices they make. Choices have consequences: Good or bad. Spiritual moral conscience must be taught in the family. Too many American children are growing up in single parent families. This is a monumental societal problem.

God is the only unifying force in the world as it is, or the world as it shall be! Moreover, death is the social equalizer regardless of any social characteristic. "And as it is appointed unto men once to die, but after this the judgment" (Hebrews 9:27). All Christians know and understand through faith: "Forever, O Lord, thy word is settled in heaven" (Psalm 119:89).

The Christian church's role in strengthening family-society spiritual unity as well as moral consciousness is extremely important as the foundation for societal unity. Unfortunately, there has been a spiritual breakdown between the family unit and the church because of materialism—material empire-building. Indeed, life without God as the foundation is senseless, and if money becomes the foundation of life, confusion abounds.

The removal of symbols of sacredness in public school environments ushered in secular humanism, and above all, devilish, inappropriate interpersonal relationships between students and students, and teachers and students. The separation of Church and State is an important political governing doctrine for obvious reasons. But all Americans should understand God's divine will for our individual as well as collective lives, because "all scripture is given by inspiration of God, and is profitable for doctrine, for reproof, for correction, for instruction in righteousness: that the man of God may be perfect, thoroughly furnished unto all good works" (2 Timothy 3:16-17).

Hypocrite in the White House

America has a President whose decadence, intellectual integrity, and moral inconsistency is historically unparalleled—except for President Andrew Jackson. In fact, being a hypocrite for some individuals is as easy as 1, 2, 3. Of course, being hypocritical is nothing new for American social democracy, because it was so, even for the founders who wrote a spiritual Preamble as well as a historic U.S. Constitution unparalleled in human history. The 45th President of these United States of America stated emphatically: "I and I alone can fix it". What a hypocritical thing to say! Currently, President Trump has surrounded himself with small-minded hypocrites who are in-fighting each other to become a "big" hypocrite, and at the same time, enslaving themselves to the super hypocrite.

"Professing themselves to be wise, they became fool" (Romans 1:22). America, understand this: "Fools make a mock at sin: but among the righteous there is favour" (Proverbs 14:9). Hypocrisy is a dangerous ungodly disease. This is why Jesus said: "Thou hypocrite, first cast out the beam out of thine own eye; and then shalt thy see clearly to cast out the mote out of thy brother's eye" (Matthew 7:5). On April 6th, 2017 the world witnessed an America with guided missiles and a misguided hypocritical President. So-called "Christian Right Evangelicals" who voted overwhelmingly for President Trump to become the 45th President are sinfully complicit in hypocrisy. All Americans knew who Donald J. Trump was and still is, because he told us, I am: A religious bigot, racial and ethnic bigot, xenophobic masochist, sexist pleasure seeker, and above all, a chronic habitual liar. God has warned us concerning this type of individual, and we did not heed God's word: "Blessed is the man that walketh not in the counsel of the ungodly, nor standeth in the way of sinners, nor sitteth in the seat of the scornful. But his delight is in the law of the Lord; and in his law doth he meditate day and night. And he shall be like a tree planted by the rivers of water, that bringeth forth his fruit in his season; his leaf also shall not wither; and whatsoever he doth shall prosper. The ungodly are not so: but are like the chaff which the wind driveth away. Therefore the ungodly shall not stand in the judgment, nor sinners in the congregation of the righteous. For the Lord knoweth the way of the righteous: but the way of the ungodly shall perish" (Psalms 1:1-6). Christian Right Evangelicals, you know better, but chose to not do better, because of your insatiable desire for the sinful hypocrisy of White Privilege. Moreover, Christian Right Evangelicals you only hurt yourselves, your children, and your grandchildren, and above all, you just might destroy America. America, pray that we are able to transcend the skin color of individuals and embrace individuals based upon their moral values and intellectual integrity.

For after all, the notion of White Privilege restrains America from truly being blessed by God far more than He has already blessed America, and above all, keeps America from becoming what God wants her to be. America refrain from your hypocritical ways for: "If my people, which are called by my name, shall humble themselves, and pray, and seek my face, and turn from their wicked ways; then will I hear from heaven, and will forgive their sin, and will heal their land" (2 Chronicles 7:14).

All Americans should be for America, not just for a political party. It has rightly been said: "There is not a Democratic America or a Republican America, Red America, or Blue America. There is only The United States Of America". And, every American should sing with great joy: "God Bless America, land that I love."

Vulgar Partisanship is individualized self-centered thinking; thinking that is outside of the Word of God, rather than interdependent thinking grounded in spiritual-societal unity. In any democratic society there must be creative tension between independent thinking and interdependent cooperation for the common good. However, it is independent partisan thinking that is causing the disintegration of America, and its two-party political system, and above all, destroying the common good. Couple this social fact with the lack of competitiveness in the drawing of congressional political lines based primarily upon cultural-ethnic sameness and what you have is mass political-governing confusion that is the masses fighting over the scraps from the table of the rich and famous. "For God is not the author of confusion, but of peace, as in all churches of the saints" (1 Corinthians 14:33). More importantly, there is ungodly anger in American society that is being fueled by lack of competitiveness in the drawing of congressional lines, income inequality, and the prominence of multiculturalism (White Privilege). Now, political partisanship governance chaos has spilled over into our religious institutions—especially Christianity because of the so-called Christian Right Evangelical Movement. And, The Supreme Court is now no longer about the Constitution and Laws, but how ultra-conservative or how ecularly-humanistically-progressive the Supreme Court Justice can interpret the LAW. Therefore, the Party affiliation of the President making Supreme Court appointments has become far more important than democratic governance of these United States of America.

Jesus said it best: "Woe unto you, scribes and Pharisees, hypocrites! For ye pay tithe of mint and anise and cumin, and have omitted the weightier matters of the law, judgment, mercy, and faith: these ought ye to have done, and not to leave the other undone. Ye blind guides, which strain at a gnat, and swallow a camel" (Matthew 23:23-24). Jesus condemned those who presented themselves as outwardly holy (righteous), but inwardly full of corruption and greed for money.

As a voice crying in the wilderness of spiritual ignorance, America get right with GOD before it is too late because the "wheels of justice grind ever so slowly, but ever so fine," Justice is a spiritual concept, but "evil men understand not judgment: but they that seek the Lord understand all things. Better is the poor that walketh in his uprightness, than he that is perverse in his ways" (Proverbs 28:5-6). "God judgeth the righteous, and God is angry with the wicked every day" (Psalm 7:11). Selah!

GOOD MEN TAKE A MORAL STAND

Every American should understand that we are in a monumental spiritual, moral crisis, whereby too many Americans are attempting to make wrong right and make it work. This approach to harmonious living with God, others, and nature is a spiritually disastrous formula for any civilized democratic society. Listening is a godly quality, and a refusal to listen to sound spiritual doctrine invariably leads to a loss of spiritual hearing and moral understanding. "Therefore to him that knoweth to do good, and doeth it not, to him it is sin" (James 4:17).

American society is at a spiritual, moral line of demarcation, and it appears as though we are about to crossover into oblivion, especially as it relates to presidential political leadership. If so-called Christian right evangelicals do not come to their spiritual faithful teachings sense based upon Biblical doctrines, we could lose it all. Currently, too many Evangelicals have itchy ears and are now chasing after fables and false, divisive doctrines. "For the time will come when they will not endure sound doctrine; but after their own lusts shall they heap to themselves teachers, having itching ears; and they shall turn away their ears from the truth, and shall be turned unto fables" (2 Timothy 4:3-4). This is already the circumstance with President Trump. Evangelicals, do not allow this to happen to you!

There are some things that should not be legislated; and, of course, this is why God gave us free will. Moreover, God has already legislated morality in the Ten Commandments. Without a doubt, the Ten Commandments are all the laws we need. Unfortunately, most individuals cannot live by them; thus, they look to thousands of man-made laws instead.

It has become vividly clear that America needs to elect more God-fearing women to political offices. Question: Why? It seems as though, in the twenty-first century, women appear to be more conscience-oriented and spiritually sensitive to the will of God that tells us to love one another. Too many men have abandoned the fortitude to embrace the will of God, and have seemingly embraced their own selfish wills for the love of power, money, and sex. Seemingly, too many men have lost their praise for God's glory; but, glorify themselves in the love of self, power, money, and sex. PMS (emotional thinking) among women only lasts for a day or two days. On the other hand, PMS that is emotional thinking among most men appears to be a permanent state of being, not a temporary condition. By the way, in case you did not know it, PMS emotional thinking among men is grounded in the love of power, money, and sex, not the love of God.

Evidently, too many Republican men in political power positions are dealing with Trumpian-Style-Feelings rather than sound spiritual doctrine based upon spiritual, moral facts and truths. They have an ungodly love affair with alternative facts (lies). Going along in order to get along is a hellish condition that is attempting to make wrong, right, and right, wrong. These so-called political leaders are tearing down the spiritual-moral tenets of American social democracy and its institutions. Consequently, American society is experiencing a monumental crisis of presidential leadership fueled by spiritually hellish Christian Right Evangelicals. Everyone that says "Lord, Lord" does not have LORD in them. "There is therefore now no condemnation to them which are in Christ Jesus, who walk not after the flesh, but after the Spirit. For the law of the Spirit of life in Christ Jesus hath made me free from the law of sin and death. For what the law could not do, in that it was weak through the flesh, God sending his own Son in the likeness of sinful flesh, and for sin, condemned sin in the flesh: that the righteousness of the law might be fulfilled in us, who walk not after the flesh, but after the Spirit" (Romans 8:1-4).

Evangelicals, you need to learn godly patience and spiritual discipline according to the Word of God. "For we are saved by hope: but hope that is seen is not hope: for what a man seeth, why doth he yet hope for [Greed, Envy, and Jealousy]? But if we hope for that we see not, then do we with patience wait for it" (Romans 8:24-25). Evangelicals, you must first understand and accept sound spiritual doctrine in order to receive this spiritual message. Moreover, please share this spiritual message with President Donald J. Trump! All hope is not godly hope. Some hope is of physical sight and "vanity of the flesh." President Trump's false "hope" that FBI Director Comey could see his way clear to cease investigating General Flynn is sinful, false-hope. God-fearing American taxpayers are hoping for the opportunity to review President Trump's income tax returns because his tax returns will reveal precisely who he truly serves: America, himself, Russia, China, Saudi Arabia or other foreign nations?

America, know full well that: "We are saved by hope: but hope that is seen is not hope: for what a man seeth, why doth he yet hope for? But if we hope for that we see not, then do we with patience wait for it" (Romans 8:24-25). President Trump supporters, if you can see it with your physical sight, it is truly vanity of the flesh, not spiritual hope.

There are demonic fleshly forces (Power, Money, and Sex) that love operating in high places that are diligently working against the Holy Bible as well as America's sacred preamble to the U.S. Constitution: "We hold these Truths to be self-evident, that all men are created equal..." All Americans understand this word of God: "What shall we then say to these things? If God be for us, who can be against us?" (Romans 8:31). More importantly, "We know that all things work together for good to them that love God, to them who are the called according to his purpose" (Romans 8:28). President Trump, Evangelicals, Republican and Democratic Partisans, and middle of the road Independents who pledge their loyalty to sinful flesh and man-made sinful institutions above God's unrestricted love for us, please understand this word of God: "For I am persuaded, that neither death, nor life, nor angels, nor principalities, nor powers, nor things to come, nor height, nor death, nor any other creature, shall be able to separate us from the love God, which is in Christ Jesus our Lord" (Romans 8: 38-39). Selah!

TO CLASSIFY: TO DECLASSIFY

To classify or to declassify sensitive national security information is the Question of Questions? Since January 20th, 2017, American society has experienced perpetual stuck-on-stupid emanating from The White House. But, more importantly, the white voters, especially the Christian Evangelicals, are guilty of electing President Donald J. Trump, a very immoral man, to the highest office in the world. To be sure, Donald J. Trump boldly told the world in his own words exactly who he is, and what he stands for, and made no bones about it! Moreover, we do not have to go into a dialogue about race. Because we all know that "RACE" still matters in America, and will probably continue to matter until Jesus returns. This is the truth, the whole truth, and nothing but the TRUTH. Most assuredly, Black America, you had best remember this social fact because there is no way to get around this socio-economic fact of American life. God's reality is different from that of President Trump's Alternative Facts Alternative Reality (LIES). The melting-pot theory is God's reality. But, seemingly, the desire of most White males is to disguise and perpetuate socio-economic inequality (White Privilege), rather than God's reality that equal is equal, not more or less equal. Just maybe, this is the biological reason why Blacks have not been permitted to really get in the melting-pot.

Donald J. Trump is against minorities, against the Islamic Religion, and against women regardless of skin color. More importantly, President Trump is against God as well as himself, and birds of a feather flock together. President Donald J. Trump has openly displayed that he has a disease called malnutrition of the brain. In fact, America's democratic institutions are under policy and procedural assault by Trump Administration officials. The lack of trustworthiness regarding statements emanating from White House officials is spiritually and morally horrifying. So much so that what began as an unpleasant joke is now a full-blown nightmare at 1600 Pennsylvania Avenue; hence, a horrifying national disaster is knocking on America's front door! For, without a doubt, America has an ungodly loose-lipped President. It has rightly been said that "loose lips sink ships." Thus, every American ought to know that when it has a President that not only has loose lips, but a severe case of malnutrition of the brain, the very nature of America's democratic institutions are endangered. For example, boastfully bragging to Russian officials in the Oval Office about firing FBI Director Comey is insane. This is vividly highlighted to the general public since seventeen different national security agencies concluded that the Russians interfered in America's Presidential election. Therefore, firing FBI director Comey was disrespectful to all Americans. Thank God for those members of the Trump Administration who love country more than power and money.

America has elected a Presidential Administration that is without godly conscience. It seems apparent that the Trump administration does have devilish tendencies and self-serving instincts which are designed to create socio-economic conditions for winners and losers —a zero-sum game. However, in a democratic society everyone should win because of the very equalitarian nature of social democracy. Only in dictatorial-communistic societies does one see structural winners and losers. The love of power and money will invariably put a hole in an individual's soul. This is why the authoritarian-dictatorial instincts of President Trump cause him to project his personal inadequacies and insecurities upon others like blaming the Victim. Therefore, the truth about President Trump's moral character, intellectual inadequacies, corrupt motives, and immoral actions are defined as fake news. However, we all know that dealing in lies is the cornerstone of fake news. Hence, in the mind of President Trump, a search for the truth is a Witch Hunt, simply because he does not want the American people to know the truth about him. Therefore, when the media tells the truth about him, he vehemently declares "Fake News." After all, and in reality, President Trump does not know how to be President of the greatest social democracy the world has ever known; nor, is he capable of intellectually disciplining himself to learn the nuances of the position. Hence, reality does not matter to Trump White House Administrative Officials, because they have been programmed and ordered to create "Alternative Facts." Moreover, part of the loyalty oath is not only loyalty to President Trump, but loyalty to telling "Alternative Facts." We all know that "Alternative Facts" are grounded in day-time fantasies and nighttime delusions without grandeur.

President Trump is a masterful, artful professional at projecting personality characteristics on to others that rightfully are more applicable and appropriate descriptions of him. For example, the Trump campaign battle cry: Crooked Hillary: Lock Her Up. The Donald J. Trump battle-cry is most appropriate in the General Flynn case: Taking the "Fifth Amendment" is an admission of criminal guilt. Needless to say, six bankruptcies and a recent cash settlement of $25 million to former students of Trump University is the epitome of crookedness. To quote Former President William J. Clinton, "Give Me a Break." We all know that Hillary is definitely not crazy. On the other hand, President Trump is publicly displaying that he is both crooked as well as crazy. Let's not ignify President Trump's description of former FBI Director Comey as a showman and a nut-job. Question: Can a spiritually blind, ditch-digging leader lead a Great Nation? I don't think so, because the Bible declares: "Let them alone: they be blind leaders of the blind. And if the blind lead the blind, both shall fall in the ditch" (Matthew 15:14). America is in a ditch because truth and reality does not matter to President Trump nor does it seem to matter to his Christian Evangelical Supporters.

Of course, in order to remain in office or to be re-elected, President Trump must initiate a war. However, weapons of war do not solve problems, because war is not the answer. This is why Jesus said unto Peter, "Put up again thy sword into its place: for all that take the sword shall perish by the sword" (Matthew 26:52). Someone needs to remind President Trump that the overwhelming majority of individuals who leveled the Twin Towers (9/11) came from Saudi Arabia, not Iran. The multi-billion-dollar arms deal to Saudi Arabia is a business deal for the wealthy business class, not a national security deal for America. All faithful Christians know that everyone that says "Lord, Lord" does not mean it. "Not everyone that saith unto me, Lord, Lord, shall enter into the Kingdom of heaven; but he that doeth the will of my Father" (Matthew 7:21). Selah!

WOULD YOU BELIEVE THIS?

The Democratic National Committee's mainframe (DNC) was hacked by the Russians and the information was publicly disseminated by Wikileaks, and seventeen different national security agencies confirmed the Russian hacking. John Podesta, Hillary Clinton's presidential campaign manager's email account was also hacked by the Russians. I, just like most of you, read and saw the news reports. But, would you believe this? I am a victim of Russian hacking. The Russians have hacked this editorial writer's email account.

I have published a number of Christian and sociologically oriented books: Corporate Christianity, Let the Church Be the Church, Transcending the Color Line, Socio-Religious Essays On American Society, Family-based Christianity, Christian Leadership: The Missing Link. And, recently I published a book of essays on the 2016 presidential election: American Society: Upside Down. The Russians did not hack my email account prior to the publication of the book of essays on the 2016 presidential election, published by St. Paul Press, Dallas. I wonder why? I could not believe that I had been hacked by Russians, and after receiving formal verification from SBC Global, my email carrier, that I indeed had been hacked by Russians, I immediately filed cyber-crime reports with the local police authority as well as the Cyber Crime Division of the FBI. I guess it's true what they say, "The pen is mightier than the sword."

I am a former Texas Southern University sociology professor and an ordained Baptist minister. I wrote a book of provocative spiritually-based essays on the 2016 presidential election, and, lo and behold, the Russians hacked my email account from eighteen different IP addresses in Russia. Question: Is it because of the book on the 2016 Presidential election? For after all, the book is about Putin's friend Donald J. Trump. Question: Does Putin have President Trump's back? For I know, without a doubt, that in Russia freedom of speech does not exist. There is only the totalitarian suppression of ideas and any form of political dissent. Readers, I pray that you have my back, because I will continue to write and speak the truth of God in Jesus' name, because equal is equal, not more or less equal. God hates racism and God-fearing Christians ought to as well. Moreover, there is no such animal as alternative facts. Truth is truth.

President Trump used the millions of dollars of inheritance from his father's estate to game and misuse white working-class individuals and our political system. He employed street-tactics to acquire up-man-ship on fifteen gentleman-like primary opponents as well as one lady primary opponent. Employing theatrics and bold-faced lies, Donald J. Trump became the standard bearer of the Republican Party. As a matter of fact, Donald J. Trump used the same street-tactics to dispatch with Hillary Clinton, the standard-bearer of the Democratic Party, with some assistance from Russian hacking intervention. In the end, President Trump lost the popular vote by almost 3 million, but was elected to the presidency according to the legality of the Electoral College System. Without a doubt, a win is a win. No doubt about it, Donald J. Trump is the 45th President of these United States of America. But, the Trump Administration is taking American society from truth to trash, from faith to fables, and in the middle of the confusion is alternative facts. This is why it is so spiritually-morally troubling that 81% of so-called Christian Evangelicals voted for Donald J. Trump, especially in a nation founded upon Christian biblical principles such as "In God We Trust." Believe me, the Trump Administration utilizing alternative facts and bold-faced lies are attempting to place American society in spiritual bondage to the love of money and lies (alternative facts).

American society is spiritually and morally upside down because one political party is seeking to perpetuate the extremism of racism based upon White Privilege. And, the other major political party desires to perpetuate the extremism of secular humanism based upon Civil rights. Sin is not a Civil Rights issue. God hates sin. Sin is a God issue (separation from God). To add fuel to the fire, Institutional Christianity has abrogated its role as the moral arbiter in society, because the church goes along to get along for the love of money, selling out the souls of individuals for the love of power and money.

Life is not about extremism, but the in-between. Life is about what is at the center of all things: God. Behold the testimony of the prophet Ezekiel who clearly understood the holiness of God. The pressures of life can orient some individuals to focus solely upon the here and now, and therefore, forget about God and His holiness. This is precisely what President Trump has done to a large segment of the American population turning them into "right now Trump automatons." "Take heed, and beware of covetousness: for a man's life consisteth not in the abundance of the things which he possesseth" (Luke 12:15).

Ezekiel's testimony about the reality of God, life, and living is recorded in the book of Ezekiel, chapter one. For Christian Evangelicals sometimes reality is not always as it seems, President Donald J. Trump is not the "wheel in the middle of a wheel." Only God can fix it. If you do not believe me, believe your own eyes; behold the uncomfortable demeanor of President Donald J. Trump worshipping in the Washington National Cathedral the day after he was sworn in as the 45th President of the United States of America. Parenthetically, I might add Presidents George H.W. Bush and President George W. Bush were comfortable in church settings. Wake-up, America, and fret not: "The earth is the Lord's, and the fullness thereof; the world, and they that dwell therein" (Psalm 24:1). Therefore, simply do as King David did: ask God to "shew me thy ways, O Lord; teach me thy paths" (Psalm 25:4). But, more importantly, remember that "God judgeth the righteous, and God is angry with the wicked every day" (Psalm 7:11). Lastly, in times like these, this day and every day, do like Enoch, walk with God, and be taken up to heaven, rather than saying "Lord, Lord," and running with the devil. Look up, America, and behold the reality of God, and stop looking to man to fix it. And, above all, America, "whatsoever ye do, do it heartily, as to the Lord, and not unto men; knowing that of the Lord ye shall receive the reward of the inheritance: for ye serve the Lord Christ" (Colossians 3:23-25). Because, "The steps of a good man are ordered by the Lord: and he delighted in his way" (Psalm 37:23). Selah!

WHEN A MALE IS NOT A MAN!

Jesus told Peter in the Gospel of Matthew, "Put up again thy sword into his place: for all they that take the sword shall perish with the sword" (Matthew 26:52). Some God-fearing individual(s) should tell the forty-fifth President of the United States Donald J. Trump and Secretary of State Rex Tillerson that war is not the answer. "He that keepeth his mouth keepeth his life: but he that openeth wide his lips shall have destruction" (Proverbs 13:3). After all, "Death and life are in the power of the tongue: and they that love it shall eat the fruit thereof" (Proverbs 18:21). But, more importantly, "The wisdom of the prudent is to understand his (God's) way: but the folly of fools is deceit" (Proverbs 14:8). For after all, "Fools make a mock of sin: but among the righteous there is favor" (Proverbs 14:9).

My fellow Americans, in order to be an effective leader, an individual must pray for wisdom, because from wisdom comes a good understanding, and from a good spiritual understanding comes knowledge. It appears that President Trump suffers from a lack of holy knowledge because no individual should answer a fool according to his folly, unless he wants to become like unto him. Moreover, "The fear of the LORD is the beginning of knowledge: but fools despise wisdom and instruction" (Proverbs 1:7). Again, "He that keepeth his mouth keepeth his life: but he that openeth wide his lips shall have destruction" (Proverbs 13:3).

The so-called Christian Evangelicals who voted for this unholy President must now vehemently tell President Trump, "Trust in the Lord with all thine heart; and lean not unto thine own understanding. In all thy ways acknowledge him, and he shall direct thy paths" (Proverbs 3:5-6). Know full well, Trump supporters, that there is no room in the inn, even for your parents, grandparents, children, and grandchildren. President Trump is about "Building Barns to Make the Rich, Richer" through military expenditures that are cutting the safety-net from under the needy in order to help the greedy. Jesus warned us about this ungodly spiritual mentality in high places in the Gospel according to Matthew: "The ground of a certain rich man brought forth plentifully: and he thought within himself, saying, What shall I do, because I have no room where to bestow my fruits? And he said, this will I do: I will pull down my barns, and I will say to my soul, Soul, thou hast much goods laid up for many years; take thine ease, eat, drink, and be merry. But God said unto him, Thou fool, this night thy soul shall be required of thee: then whose shall those things be, which thou hast provided? So is he that layeth up treasure for himself, and is not rich toward God" (Matthew 12:16-21). America, is President Trump "the Second Coming"? After all, he has declared that only he can fix it! Or just maybe it is the other way around: "F—K it up?

When a male is not a man and has an institutional power leadership role, individuals have HELL to contend with. Furthermore, your sons and daughters are in imminent danger! Moreover, when the Secretary of State is on foreign soil talking war indirectly to an insane KRAZY-MAD-MAN-FOREIGN-LEADER with nuclear power capabilities and has the killer spirit of Cain who killed his uncle, recently had his own brother killed, and touts Dennis Rodman as a foreign policy advisor, the world community is indeed in deep trouble spiritually and physically. More importantly, any individual that follows a vain person is void of spiritual knowledge and understanding. After all, "The way of a fool is right in his own eyes: but he that hearkeneth unto counsel is wise" (Proverbs 12:15). It is moral character, intellectual integrity, and the ability to confess mistakes to others that makes a male a man, not dogmatic stubbornness.

Question: What is the nature of the collaborative power conspiracy between the Trump Administration, Putin, and the Russian government all about? America needs to know. For after all, it appears to be of evil intent, not about godly intent for either their respective countries or the world community. By the way, some males are victimized by PMS: Power, Money, and Sex.

Only God is perfect in goodness; not individuals, whether male or female. Again, when America's Chief Diplomat is on foreign soil making war talk, rather than peace, indirectly to an insane foreign adversarial leader, we now know why he didn't want the position, but accepted the position when asked. This type of leadership mentality is neither godly nor manly in character, but foolhardy. The primary role of Secretary of State is world peace-keeping initiatives through diplomatic channels, not threatening war. War is never the answer. Jesus is the answer. More importantly, strategies for peace-keeping should initially be discussed in State department staff meetings. Maybe this is why Secretary Tillerson chooses not to meet on a regular basis with the staff of the State Department, or chooses not to have the National Press core travel with him, and does not participate in Presidential Cabinet level meetings. Maybe the Trump Administration's "Foreign Policy Objective" is to wage war, not keep the peace. Perhaps this is the explanation for the gutting of the federal budget in order to increase military spending by $54 billion! Without a doubt, the leadership conflict story of David and King Saul is a classic example of what godly leadership is all about (1 Samuel 24:1-22)! King David hated lying because "a righteous man hateth lying: but a wicked man is loathsome, and cometh to shame" (Proverbs 13:5).

A federal budget is a set of national priorities. Is the Trump administration's priority singularly to utilize the federal budget through military expenditures as a blueprint designed simply to make the rich, richer, and the poor, poorer?

Life is truly not about extremes, but the in-between (center). The prophet Ezekiel discovered the reality of God as the "wheel in the middle of wheels" that makes everything go around (Ezekiel 1:16-21). President Trump thinks of himself as a big wheel and a shot-caller, but one day he will discover that God is the "little-big-wheel" at the center of all wheels that makes everything go around. A real man knows that "the way of a fool is right in his own eyes: but he that followeth vain persons is void of understanding" (Proverbs 12:11). Trump supporters, a spiritual word to the wise ought to be sufficient, because: "There is that maketh himself rich, yet hath nothing: there is that maketh himself poor, yet hath great riches" (Proverbs 13:7). Regrettably, there are some males who love power and material riches (money) more so than family, friends, or country. Selah!

Political Party Interests or National Interests

Abraham Lincoln said it best: "A nation divided against itself cannot stand!" The very nature of democracy as a political governing system of check and balances is about compromising on methods of how to obtain the universal common good, not compromising moral values and spiritual principles. This is why American society has three equal branches of governmental power.

An individual cannot convince a fool against his own will not to be a fool. Therefore, only a fool can identify with another fool. This is why the Bible emphatically states: "Answer not a fool according to his folly, lest thou also be like unto him" (Proverbs 26:4). Fellow Americans, God is a promise keeper and Donald Trump is a promise maker/breake with no good intentions, but his own. "But as it is written, Eye hath not seen, nor ear heard, neither have entered into the heart of man, the things which God hath prepared for them that love him" (1 Corinthians 2:9). To be an American or not to be an American is the question? Donald Trump is not capable of intellectually, mentally, and morally understanding the role of the Presidency of the United States of America. And, above all, understand that America's birth is grounded in multiculturalism.

The 2016 presidential election has absolutely nothing to do with

Donald Trump, but everything to do with the American public, especially Trump supporters. Everybody should understand who Trump is; especially if you have ears to hear, eyes to see, a mind to think, and a heart to know the truth. This editorial is going somewhere; therefore, for the sake of American society, go with me. At this time, America is the greatest nation on the earth. But, the spin-masters (the press and Trump followers) would have the American people believe that nothing is right with America. Therefore, elect Trump and "Make America Great Again." It's all about JOBS, and the American Dream, which is a suburban home, two cars, and a college education for their children. But, we all know, especially Trump followers, that it is also about White Privilege and institutional Racism.

However, even in our wildest imagination(s) no one would have believed the recent Trump sexist revelations, the verba sexual antics, and physical abuse of women openly joked about in the recent video clip (October 7, 2016). In recent years Americans, especially Black Americans have admired, respected, and even praised Bill Cosby for his humanitarianism and dramatic genius as an entertainer. But, when forty or more women brought to the attention of the American public that they were sexually violated by Bill Cosby many individuals said he should be placed on trial, convicted, and placed in jail. Yet, Bill Cosby has never indicated publicly that he desired to become the leader of the free-world. Donald Trump, in the video seen on October 7th, with the promise of potentially more to come, proves one indisputable point: Trump is a first class low life representing an outraged cultural dimension of American society, and as a consequence has made America the joke of the free world. Trump

90

represents a vulgar unsophisticated form of white privilege in the most pluralistic, multicultural society in the world.

Without a doubt, Trump is morally bankrupt and intellectually unfit to hold the Office of President. Talking about Former President Bill Clinton's sin is not justification for one's own sin(s). Former President Clinton has paid for his sins; he was impeached, lost his law license, paid a monetary fine, and apologized to the American people. But, more importantly, Bill Clinton is not on the November 8th ballot. The second Presidential debate was an international disgrace before both God and the world community made so by Donald Trump with his physical stalking and verbal antics. Trump attempted to BOLDLY defend and justify his sin rather than asking for godly forgiveness and stepping down in his pursuit of attempting to become the leader of the free world. All God has asked of every individual is: "Let us therefore come boldly unto the throne of grace, that we may obtain mercy, and find grace to help in time of need" (Hebrews 4:16). The Trumpster cannot even do that; in his heart he wants to play God; therefore please remember he said that he has 'nothing to ask God to forgive him for.' And, "For as he thinketh in his heart, so is he: Eat and drink, saith he to thee, but his heart is not with thee" (Proverbs 23:7). Remember, America, his heart is not with thee. It is not our responsibility to judge the Trumpster, but we can try to morally understand his behavior. Christian supporters of the Donald please pray with him and for him, and above all, meditate upon this verse: "For what shall it profit a man, if he shall gain the whole world, and lose his own soul?" (Mark 8:36).

The "Children of Cain," who appear to be Republican Party malcontents, who are obviously looking for something for nothing. There is no shame in their game. However, Christian Evangelicals ought to be truly doubly ashamed of placing Party political interests above national interests and family values. Republican National Leadership, because of Trump's support from malcontents, and in conjunction with the national press for TV ratings based upon Trump's repulsive antics, and his language-style for TV ratings (commercial value) created the elephant in the room. Without a doubt, there were highly intellectually capable Governors involved in the primary selection process. Yet, Donald Trump was allowed to trash-talk these highly qualified individuals out of the Primary process. Shame! Shame! Shame! To be sure, the 2016 Presidential election is emphatically not about Donald Trump, but the children of Cain (The Cain Generation). Cain killed his brother Abel. And, God asked Cain: Where is thy brother? And, Cain "questioned" God, and asked: "Am I my brother's keeper?" (Genesis 4:8-13). Yes, Donald, you are your brother's keeper, as well as your sister's keeper, and every individual has a mother.

Donald Trump and Trump-followers, Be Careful: "Be not deceived; God is not mocked: for whatsoever a man soweth, that shall he reap. For he that soweth to his flesh shall of the flesh reap corruption; but he that soweth to the Spirit shall of the Spirit reap life everlasting" (Galatians 6:7-8). Finally, my fellow Americans, and above all, Republican-malcontents: "Be not deceived: evil communications corrupt good manners. Awake to righteousness, and sin not; for some have not the knowledge of God: I speak this to your shame" (1 Corinthians 15:33-34). Selah!

The Southern Strategy is Destroying the Republican Party

The seed-bed for the Southern strategy was birthed in 1964 with the advent of Senator Barry Goldwater's presidential aspirations. The strategy reached its apex under the Presidential leadership of Ronald Reagan. Seemingly, the Republican Party's "Southern Strategy" is based upon perpetuating White Privilege while it continues to perpetuate minority subjugation. Without a doubt, the "Southern Strategy" has created political stagnation (polarization) in our national governmental system.

American society has become a spiritual vision written in a profound document (U.S. Constitution) rather than a living spiritual reality. Make no mistake about it, the problem is the profound desire on the part of some Whites to perpetuate White Privilege. In 2015, if you are White, an individual can come to America stay for six months, apply for citizenship, and become successful overnight. The U.S. Constitution states very clearly that if you are born in America you are an American citizen. And, at the same time, some Republicans want to declare that so-called "anchor babies" must return to the country of origin of their parents; even though the Constitution states otherwise. While, on the other hand, no matter what an individual can or cannot contribute to American society, seemingly if the individual is White he is right, if Black get back, and if Brown stick around (color-line-distinctions). But, above all, toe the line. This is not written in law, but sublingual language.

America is on a downhill descent with a hard right drag. Obstructionism is a political philosophy that declares that it is "my way or the highway." The Presidential debates reveal clearly how destructive the "Southern Strategy" has become to America's political well-being. Simply because when men and one woman of the same political party (persuasion) cannot get along with each other (civility), then minorities do not stand a ghost of a chance. Therefore, America is structurally functioning against its own well-being socio-politically and economically, but more importantly, spiritually and morally. At the center of this societal free-fall is political partisanship gridlock (obstructionism).

The Democratic Party is destroying the moral fabric of American society by attempting to make every issue an issue of civil rights. The Republican Party is destroying the civility of American society with notions of White Privilege, and a misguided, devilish interpretation of the Second Amendment to the U.S. Constitution, thereby engendering a vulgar gun culture. It is written: "Where there is no vision, the people perish: but he that keepth the law, happy is he" (Proverbs 29:18). Woe unto those who interfere with the well-being of children of God, because if God has to straighten out your mess, you probably will not like the results. "And I will bring the blind by a way that they knew not; I will lead them in paths that they have not known: I will make darkness light before them, and crooked things straight. These things will I do unto them, and not forsake them" (Isaiah 42:16).

I pray that as a nation-state we do not spiritually embrace the destructiveness of a haughty heart because: "Before destruction the heart of a man is haughty; and before honor is humility" (Proverbs 18:12). But, let us with humility receive the honor of God's glory for future generations.

America must learn to keep the two great commandments of Jesus: "Love the Lord thy God with all thy heart, and with all thy soul, and with thy entire mind. This is the first and great commandment. And the second is like unto it, Thou shalt love thy neighbor as thyself" (Matthew 22:37-39). America is truly void of visionary political leadership.

Society begins and ends in the family unit. Men must be able to provide for the basic survival needs of their families (food, shelter, and clothing). God said that a man must work (Genesis 3:17-19). Therefore, work is God's gift to men, and of course the work of men should be oriented toward commitment: "Commit thy works unto the Lord, and thy thoughts shall be established. The Lord hath made all things for himself" (Proverbs 16:3-4). But, above all, "Thou art worthy, O Lord, to receive glory and honor and power: for thou hast created all things, and for thy pleasure they are and were created" (Revelation 4:11). Apparently, some men (White and Black) in both political parties did not get the e-mail message or text message because some are still implementing the southern strategy (sin) and same-sex-marriage (sin), because sin is a free-will human right, not a civil rights issue. Or, if they did, they deleted the message.

Unfortunately, there are still in play racist institutional structural impediments that keep Black men from acquiring meaningful work (employment) in American society. The key to a vibrant economic system (economic growth) is growing JOBS (meaningful work). By the way, the system does not want full employment that is zero unemployment. This is why full-employment is defined as (3-4) percent of the potential White American workforce unemployed, because structurally the system is not designed to produce full-employment (zero unemployment). A job (work) gives glory to God and self-pride and self-gratification to individuals, especially men. In the past, the Southern strategy was about slave labor. In the twenty-first century, the Southern strategy is about illegal immigrant labor.

The Grand Ole Party (Party of Abraham Lincoln) has become the party of Ronald Reagan that is the ole Democrat Party of the South (Dixiecrats). Sometimes the more things change the more they remain the same.

But, "Let us therefore come boldly unto the throne of grace, that we may obtain mercy, and find grace to help in time of need" (Hebrews 4:16). Amen!

SHAME! SHAME! SHAME!

On November 8th, 2016, the American people elected a bigoted, xenophobic, sexist, racist, masochist, religious bigot, and above all, a wealthy businessman without a common touch to the Office of the President. Out of the 300 million Americans, the American electorate chose Donald J. Trump to be the President of these United States of America. Shame! Shame! Shame! But, more importantly, President Trump is also representing the image of democratic leadership of the "free world." Shame! Shame! Shame! It has been said, and it is a profound truth: "Elections Have Consequences." The election of Donald J. Trump to the Office of President is a consequence that neither America nor the world needed! Shame! Shame! Shame!

Unfortunately, most of America's institutions as we know them today will invariably be changed negatively, not positively. When the President does not believe in, nor trust America's National Security Intelligence Agencies, we have a monumental national security problem. Question: Whose intelligence does President Trump trust? Or does the President lean toward his own misguided understanding? "Trust in the Lord with all thine heart; and lean not unto thine own understanding. In all thy ways acknowledge him, and he shall direct thy paths" (Proverbs 3:5-6). Shame! Shame! Shame!

American society is experiencing a spiritual-moral crisis of presidential leadership unlike any other in its history. Getting elected to the office of President does not necessarily mean that you are a qualified moral leader. In fact, America's current presidential leadership mentality is that of a Third World Nation that is a graveyard dictatorial mentality and one that is not befitting of the most spiritually enlightened democracy on the planet. Presidential leadership is about character, morality, intellectual integrity, and spiritual conscience, not political chicanery. Shame! Shame! Shame!

A Free Press is the spiritual-moral-intellectual foundation of social democracy, and without a Free Press a nation devolves into a dictatorial societal structure. Checks and balances are extremely important in any civilized society, especially a democratic society. God has already given us a blue-print for a moral society. "The Lord gave the word: great was the company of those that published it" (Psalms 68:11). The presidential declaration of "Fake News" and that the Press is the enemy of the American people is a diversionary tactic designed to cover-up (deflect) political-economic corruption, and at the same time, create an atmosphere for White Nationalism subliminally suggesting that America was built by Whites for Whites. And, now America is too multi-cultural on the Black-side. Without a doubt, this is an absolute bald face lie. America was built on the backs of free slave labor. If you do not believe me, I beseech you to visit the National Civil Rights Museum in Washington, D.C., and above all, read the dedicatory speech of former President George W. Bush on September 24th, 2016. Shame! Shame! Shame!

Question: Why was Donald J. Trump elected to the office of the Presidency? The answer to the question is "confirmation-bias" because there are a lot of Americans who simply believe what they want to believe, even though it is not grounded in the reality of the TRUTH. For example, the rationale of many individuals that voted for President Trump was the false promise of high paying jobs—jobs that require high levels of skills, as well as technical training, not a high school diploma. In fact, the jobs that have been outsourced to foreign countries can be performed by any individual with minimal formal levels of education because the jobs are based upon non-skilled repetition. Shame! Shame! Shame!

Time marches on and twenty-first century technological progress doesn't wait on any individual. Everything must change and nothing remains the same. Therefore, living in the past with notions of White Privilege on your mind is a recipe for national disaster. America is a multi-cultural society, like it or not. Moreover, it is what it is. Therefore, White males, stop crying and complaining, get technically trained, because you know better and want better; therefore, do better. Work is the gift of God to man as well as family (Genesis 3:17-19). For after all, in the Black community, the family structure has been literally destroyed because of the inability of too many Black men to acquire meaningful work. And, we all know who is responsible for these societal conditions. All Americans should prayerfully embrace this scripture: "Learn to do well; seek judgment, relieve the oppressed, judge the fatherless, plead for the widow" (Isaiah 1:17). Shame! Shame! Shame!

What is spiritually troubling about the election of Donald J. Trump to the Office of President is the percentage of White female voters, both college educated and non-college educated who voted for him, especially after, in his own words, he vividly described his disrespect for women on the Billy Bush video tape. Of course, "Every way of man is right in his own eyes, but the Lord pondereth the hearts" (Proverbs 21:2). Every woman needs to spiritually understand that she is a free interdependent moral being, because "ye are of God, little children, and have overcome them: because greater is he that is in you, than he that is in the world" (1 John 4:4). God created a woman; when God called Eve into being Adam was sleep (Genesis 2:18-25). Therefore, it was somewhat surprising that so many White women identify with tenets of White Privilege rather than who God says they are. In the sight of God, men and women are of equal human dignity regardless of skin-color.

During Trump's political campaign, he declared Mexicans who were illegally entering America to be rapists, robbers, and killers. Moreover, some Trump-supporters have designated illegal immigrants as Illegal Aliens from some other planet, not as human beings who are hard workers, family centered, Christian-Oriented with a simple desire to work for an honest wage because of economic conditions in their countries of origin. But, we all know, that Mexicans and other Latin American Hispanics are victims of cheap labor conspiracies on the part of American Capitalism. More importantly, lest we forget, when President Trump was publicly asked about Putin being a killer, he invariably declared that America is a killer as well. Without a doubt, "Righteousness exalteth a nation: but sin is a reproach to any people." (Proverbs 14:34).

POLITICS AND STRANGE BED-PARTNERS

Donald Trump has embarked upon a scorch-societal policy. If I cannot become the President, then I will destroy American society as we know it. Without a doubt, the Trumpster already knows that he has discredited himself as a Presidential candidate. And, as a result, America's international image is tainted, due to Trump's uncivil behavior. His statement in the third debate is proof positive of his self-centered destructive mentality—when he refused to say that he would accept the final results of the 2016 Presidential election. Now, the Trumpster is flaming the fires of vigilantism just like Nero. Trump is playing on his harp based upon his privileged birth position while helping to bring America to her knees internally by sowing seeds of doubt in free, fair, and just elections. Unfortunately, the day after the debate, the Trumpster added fuel to the fire by saying: "I'll accept the results, if I win." This is the big "I" in the middle of "SIN."

Trump is manipulating non-college-educated White males whose jobs have been sent abroad by profiteering businessmen, just like Trump, whose only concern is bottom-line profits, not American families. Yet, these same working class White males have been hood-winked into believing that it is trade-policy agreements that have created the economic problem of loss of living wage jobs, not corporate greed. Working class White males need to change their spiritual and political mind-set. "I beseech you therefore, brethren, by the mercies of God, that ye present your bodies a living sacrifice, holy, acceptable unto God, which is your reasonable service. And be not conformed to this world, but be ye transformed by the renewing of your mind, that ye may prove what is that good, acceptable, and perfect, will of God" (Romans 12:1-2).

Trump followers when you choose an extremely flawed Presidential "Standard-Bearer" such as the Trumpster you have placed your children's children's lives in the balance, because they will never be able to realize the American Dream. Therefore, look at the individual in the mirror, and spiritually understand this scripture: "When he speaketh fair, believe him not: for there are seven abominations in his heart." The Biblical reference is to the the Seven Deadly Sins ("a proud look, a lying tongue, hands that shed innocent blood, a heart that deviseth wicked imaginations, feet that are swift to run to mischief, false witness that speaketh lies, and he that soweth discord among brethren"). Of course, sin is lawlessness and vanity. And, "Whose hatred is covered by deceit, his wickedness shall be shewed before the whole congregation" (Proverbs 26: 25-26). The spirit of Abraham Lincoln is probably grieved at what has happened to the Republican Party as the spiritual backbone of freedom, justice, and equality of opportunity for all Americans.

Donald Trump in his own words has told the world in no uncertain, undignified terms what he thinks of women, immigrants, and other fellow Americans. Every woman is a potential mother, and should be treated with the highest regard and respect. Therefore, I do not need to remind anyone of the spiritual-biological factor associated with motherhood. And, likewise, every man is a potential father. All Americans are duty-called to make America live up to the Preamble to the U.S. Constitution. Thus, let every American pray to our Heavenly Father (God), especially Christian Evangelicals, that most fathers do not spiritually and politically imitate the behavior of the Trumpster, because we all know that Esau tricked his brother (Jacob) out of his birthright. When all is said and done, all individuals need to spiritually understand this scripture, especially the Trumpster: "He that keepeth his mouth keepeth his life: but he that openeth wide his lips shall have destruction." (Proverbs 13: 3).

The Trumpster has boldly said from his own mouth who he is; a sexual predator, haters of minority immigrants, and fellow Americans who are not fortunate enough to be born to rich parents. By the way, we also hope and pray that potential mothers are not chasing after rainbows looking for a pot of gold that is searching for something for nothing (Gold-Diggers). We all know that nothing from nothing leave nothing. Individuals should not "judge", but should always try the Spirit by the Spirit; therefore, there is a possibility that the Donald is not capable of receiving redemption.

The Trumpster, with his unfounded, malicious allegations (habitual lying) that the 2016 presidential election is rigged, is stroking the embers of ungodly societal violence, and at the same time, is playing on the frustrations of weak-minded individuals who are capable of committing criminal acts. Of course, no other presidential election has been rigged. It's all about him! Stupid! Stupid! Stupid! Question: Why wasn't the 2008 presidential election rigged against President Obama: (Birther Movement)? And, why wasn't the 2000 election rigged against President George W. Bush since the Democratic Party was in charge of the White House? The answer to the question is simply this in American society there is a check on the checker, and above all, both political parties believe in the time-honored tradition of fair and just democratic elections. But, more importantly, both political parties believe in a smooth transition of power. (Just ask "gentleman" presidential candidate Al Gore.)

Donald Trump has no political leadership history that the American people can judge and evaluate him by. But, what he does have is a selfish business record that all Americans can evaluate and inspect, because it includes six business bankruptcies, including one for almost one billion dollars. Question: What kind of hooking-and-crooking businessman is this, because even with other people's money he fails? This is why the American people deserve to see his federal income tax returns. One thing we do know about the Trumpster is that his business ventures have left a lot of individuals holding what elephants leave on fairgrounds. Trump supporters, wake up, embrace common sense reality, and ask God's forgiveness for being so naively gullible before it is too late. Finally, Christian Evangelicals meditate on this scripture, because Trumpster has built some buildings with other people's money, but "every house is builded by some man, but he that built all things is God" (Hebrews 3:4). Our earnest prayer is that America never forgets it. Selah!

LIES! LIES! LIES!

The Bible emphatically declares that no God-fearing individual should lie: "Thou shalt not bear false witness against thy neighbor" (Exodus 20:16). It has rightly been said there are three types of lies: Lies, Damn Lies, and How to Lie Using Statistics. Of course, there are lies and more lies that come from the mouth of ungodly individuals. In fact, the Bible declares that the beginning of all sin is a LIE. "For God is not the author of confusion (LIES), but of peace, as in all churches of the saints" (1 Corinthians 14:33). More importantly, "Ye are of your father the devil, and the lusts of your father ye will do. He was a murderer from the beginning, and abode not in the truth, because there is no truth in him. When he speaketh a lie, he speaketh of his own: for he is a liar, and the father of it" (John 8:44).

President Trump is a professional, chronic, habitual liar to the nth degree at employing all three types of lies in his quest for absolute dictatorial power. Republicans have desired the Presidential power to govern for eight years, and now they have not only the Office of the President, but majorities in both the House of Representatives as well as the Senate Chamber. And, now that they have all three branches of governmental authority under their leadership, they know what they want to do: make the rich, richer and the poor, poorer. But, they can't do it because they are too busy covering up President Trump's lies. Above all, Republicans do not know how to govern with democratic fairness. Their desire is to simply govern with conservatism without spiritual, moral, and intellectual conscience and integrity. Republicanism without spiritual-moral conscience is a recipe for electing a professional liar to the Office of the President. Now, that they have it, "what in the hell" are they going to do with it? Without a doubt, President Trump has surrounded himself with a professional political director and a team of go-along-to-get-along lie-accommodators. To be sure, if it were not for a free press with intellectual-integrity, America must wonder where she would be with Donald J. Trump as President.

Republican talk is cheap. This is why President Trump declared we didn't know that healthcare was so complicated. Of course, social democracy/political governance is much more difficult to achieve in a society, because it requires equality of opportunity for all, not White Nationalistic Privilege. More than practically anything else, democracy requires political leaders that are willing to tell the truth, the whole truth, and nothing but the truth so help them God, not foster a Sanhedrin Council of automatons who are willing to become lie-accommodators. In case you are not familiar with the work of the Sanhedrin Council, remember the condemnation of Jesus.

The poor will always be with us because, invariably, the rich become greedy, and above all, the poor help to make the rich, rich. Unfortunately, the rich want more, they need more, and above all, they have to have more. "Take heed and beware of covetousness: for a man's life consisteth not in the abundance of the things which he possesseth. The ground of a certain rich man brought forth plentifully: and he thought within himself, saying, What shall I do, because I have no room where to bestow my fruits? And, he said, This will I do: I will pull down my barns, and build greater; and there will I bestow all my fruits and goods. And I will say to my soul, Soul, thou hast much goods laid up for many years; take thine ease, eat, drink, and be merry. But God said unto him, Thou fool, this night thy soul shall be required of thee: then whose shall those things be, which thou hast provided? So is he that layeth up treasure for himself, and is not rich toward God" (Luke 12:13-21). It is more profitable for an individual to have a rich relationship with God than to possess tons of silver and gold. In President Trump's mind, he wants America to be in the same trick bag he is in with Putin and Russia where they ultimately become co-dictators of the world community. This is precisely why the Secretary of State is silent and has dismissed top career professional diplomats who have been employed in the State department for more than 20 years.

Seemingly there are the first stages of a world-governing conspiracy operating between President Trump and Putin. In fact, they desire to control the human and physical resources of the world community. Putin desires to control the Eastern countries with Germany as the plum caveat. President Trump will then control the West and the rest of the world community. However, President Trump will soon discover that the East and Germany are not enough because Putin wants to control the whole world. More importantly, Putin knows that there can only be one dictator (El Supremo). "For as he thinketh in his heart, so is he: Eat and drink, saith he to thee; but his heart is not with thee" (Proverbs 23:7). For after all, President Trump will find this truism out the hard way: Because a hard head makes a soft behind. Neither President Trump nor Dictator Putin has compassion for their fellow countrymen; they only want to use their fellow countrymen as pawns in a chess game for power and material riches. Behold, America you have been told. Therefore, "Let it be written: Let it be done." Stop the madness now; unless you are insane.

God has a Sovereign Will, and He has a Permissive Will. President Donald J. Trump is a spiritual reflection of God's Permissive Will. God allowed Donald J. Trump to be elected President. God is seeking to get America's undivided attention. For after all, America is destroying itself from within because of its evil thinking about racial and ethnic superiority, its lust for power, and its insatiable love and greed for money by both political, as well as, religious leaders. "Nevertheless the foundation of God standeth sure, having this seal, The lord knoweth them that are his. And, Let everyone that nameth the name of Christ depart from iniquity" (2 Timothy 2:19). America, "Get Right: Live Right" for the time is at hand. Prepare for the judgment of God. "So then every one of us shall give account of himself to God" (Romans 14:12). Beware, therefore, of promises made by LIARS. Needless to say, God gave Noah the "rainbow sign, no more water, but the fire next time." Selah!

Religious Conservatism Versus All-White Conservatism

To be or not to be is an eternal question, because it is a question about commitment that is Children of God versus Children of Cain: Who is on the Lord's side? Without a doubt, "Before destruction the heart of man is haughty, and before honour is humility" (Proverbs 18:12). But, more importantly, "Death and life are in the power of the tongue" (Proverbs 18:21). All individuals, especially individuals who are seeking high profile public, leadership positions like that of the presidency of the United States of America, should choose their words wisely. "There is a way which seemeth right unto a man, but the end thereof are the ways of death" (Proverbs 14:12). Without a doubt, "God is not the author of confusion, but of peace, as in all the churches of the saints" (1 Corinthians 14:33). Therefore, Children of God do not create confusion, because all things must be done decently, and in order, especially in a democratic society.

If a want-to-be leader cannot live by this Holy Scripture, "But grow in grace, and in the knowledge of our Lord and Savior Jesus Christ. To him be glory both now and forever" (2 Peter 3:18), he or she does not qualify as a want-to-be-leader.

The Trump phenomenon is primarily grounded in White working class misunderstanding and racial-ethnic-socio-economic scapegoating. In fact, the Trump presidential candidacy has exposed the ugly White Privilege underbelly of the Republican Party, as well as the hypocrisy of American society as a democratic melting pot. Of course, without a doubt, the socio-economic failures of White working class Americans have nothing whatsoever to do with the existence of permanent-tan minorities in America. The system is rigged based upon the principle of White Privilege and institutional racism. And, by the way, trade agreements have little or nothing to do with the loss of skilled labor jobs, but everything to do with the financial bottom line of multinational corporations/enterprises, not federal trade policies. This is why individuals need an education in a democratic-technological-information society. By the way, individuals with guns do not alleviate the problem or the conditions of jobs going abroad. Neither does same-sex marriage create jobs, only societal confusion, because "Righteousness exalteth a nation: but sin is a reproach to any people" (Proverbs 14:34). But, we all should know, "For as he thinketh in his heart, so is he" (Proverbs 23:7).

Therefore, working class Whites need to stop whining, stop looking for privileges based upon skin color in a multi-cultural nation, stop following leaders with immoral and psychological challenges, obtain occupational retraining, obtain a quality education, and, by-and-large, meaningful employment will be available.

Nevertheless, when it is all said and done, all of us sin, and come short of the glory of God. "And as it is appointed unto men once to die, but after this the judgment" (Hebrews 9:27). Indeed, it is unfortunate that, "Fools make a mock at sin: but among the righteous there is favour" (Proverbs 14:9). And, above all, God-fearing Americans understand that "the wisdom of the prudent is to understand his (God's) way: but the folly of fools is deceit" (Proverbs 14:8).

Most individuals are conservative based upon spiritual principles, moral values, and conscience. However, Republican Conservatism has evolved into White Paranoia. In fact, it is Biblically recorded that God made man out of dirt, and breathed into his nostrils the breath of life. The last time I checked, there is no such element as white dirt. Therefore, life and death issues are not grounded in skin color, but the will of God (Matthew 22:36-40).

All White Conservatism is the only rational explanation for the rise of a Donald Trump leadership-style-personality bold enough to seek the presidency of supposedly the most sophisticated democratic nation-state in the world community? The Republican Party is an original major political party whose founding personality and godly spirit was Abraham Lincoln: "Together We Stand: Divided We Fall." In fact, the Party of Lincoln was established on the time-honored principle of justice and liberty for all, not all-White Conservatism. It is, indeed, an unfortunate set of circumstances for America (a nation of immigrants), as well as the world community, that the Republican Party since 1964 (Senator Barry Goldwater) has been marching toward a Donald Trump-style presidency.

Whites rule the world, but God rules the universe, and minorities do have a say in how Whites govern; especially in American society because of the power of the vote. Just maybe this is why voting rights are under legal attack by All-White Conservatism. Of course, at one time in America's history, voting rights were under attack legally as well as physically. The right to vote is the cornerstone sacred principle of participatory democracy. Therefore, thank God for President Lyndon B. Johnson and the Civil Rights Act of 1964 and the Voting Rights Act of 1965.

As Americans, we must right the Ship Of State, spiritually correct the course, and "Let us therefore come boldly unto the throne of grace, that we may obtain mercy, and find grace to help in time of need" (Hebrews 4:16).

March Madness

March Madness in 2017 is not about college basketball, but the Presidential leadership mentality in The White House that has produced an "April Fool's Joke" Without a doubt, this April, American society is experiencing a monumental crisis of Presidential leadership governance unlike any in its history. Moreover, America has an intellectual integrity, moral character, and conscientious leadership problem, not just a political governance problem. Getting elected does not mean that you are worthy of electability. It may simply mean that you were able to hoodwink the right-wrong thinking voters in the right electoral college states. My fellow Americans, "I beseech you therefore by the mercies of God, that ye present your bodies a living sacrifice, holy acceptable unto God, which is your reasonable service. And be not conformed to this world: but be ye transformed by the renewing of your mind, that ye may prove what is that good, and acceptable, and perfect, will of God" (Romans 1:1-2). America, it is not too late through legal channels/impeachment to throw the ungodly bums OUT of the White House; especially before they turn America over to Putin and a Russian State, without firing a shot, and destroy our democratic institutions in the process.

America, our institutional structures cannot withstand perpetual Presidential and institutional lying. Americans must be told the truth and nothing but the truth, especially from the Oval Office. "Let every soul be subject unto the higher powers. For there is no power but of God: the powers that be are ordained of God. Whosoever therefore resiseth the power, resisteth the ordinance of God: and they that resist shall receive to themselves damnation" (Romans 13: 1-2). A lie cannot stand. A lie can only deflect momentarily; until it is challenged, again and again. Truth will prevail. America, permit God to "Sanctify them through thy truth: thy word is truth" (John 17:17). "Ye shall know the truth, and the truth shall make you free" (John 8:32).

Any casual spiritual observer that understands socio-economic facts and watched the repeal-and-replace-Obamacare circus should by now clearly understand that most White males can only be in agreement when dealing with clearly defined majority-minority situations. Get over it, America! Let's build an inclusive democratic society, because we must teach our children as well as future generations how to forgive. Minorities, especially Black Americans, have forgiven the past, because the past belongs to the devil!

Some Americans, seemingly just can't get over it? Without a doubt, what is currently transpiring in American society is all about White Privilege. Because some Americans have an insatiable appetite for power and money which, in turn, drives them to sell-out America for thirty pieces of silver (foreign or domestic) which is a Biblical financial term for unethical behavior, Of course, lying and ethnic conflicts are not "Making America Great Again," but making America "Ugly America" in the spiritual eye sight of the world community. Moreover, America's intellectual integrity and spiritual-moral character foundation is being eroded (destroyed) for the sake of White

Privilege for a few Whites, and not all Whites. Simply put, greed and power does not permit room at the top for all Whites because absolute power corrupts absolutely.

As adults, we must teach and remind each other that our children are a gift from God, that the future belongs to God, that our children are our future in God for building the Kingdom of God on earth as it is in heaven, that to forgive is divine, and that they should always be peace makers. "Lo, children are an heritage of the Lord: and the fruit of the womb is his reward" (Psalms 127:3). More importantly, we must teach our children how to become peace-makers and not war-mongers, because: "Blessed are the peacemakers: for they shall be called the children of God. Blessed are the pure in heart for they shall see God. Blessed are the merciful for they shall obtain mercy. Blessed are they which do hunger and thirst after righteousness: for they shall be filled" (Matthew 5:6-9).

Forewarned is foretold. The ungodly governmental lying must stop, especially the Presidential lying, because what is at stake is the future of American society as we know it. Great nations rise and fall simply because of an immoral leader's desire to become the master of the world. Jesus is Lord and Master. "For with the heart man believeth unto righteousness; and with the mouth confession is made unto salvation" (Romans 10:10). Out of his own mouth the 45th President has dishonored himself as well as all Americans. After all, from the heart of his mind he has told us precisely how he feels about minorities, women, certain religions, and individuals with opinions different from his own.

Jesus is Lord and Master because of this scriptural verse penned by Paul: "For I say, through the grace given unto me, to every man that is among you, not to think of himself more highly than he ought to think; but to think soberly, according as God hath dealth to every man the measure of faith" (Romans 12:3). Therefore, Christian America, "Let every soul be subject unto the high powers. For there is no power but of God" (Romans 13:1). Every American, let's boldly celebrate the resurrection of Our Lord and Savior, Jesus Christ the Righteous One. Selah!

THE BLAME GAME

Blame, blame, and blame is the name of the President Trump White House Game: Oops Gang. The Trump administration is unwilling to take responsibility for their own decisions; therefore, Trump and the White House project the blame for their administrative dysfunction upon President Obama, House Minority Leader Nancy Pelosi, Senate Minority Leader Schumer or the Democratic Party in general. Above all, President Trump is a blame game specialist. Shame! Shame! Shame!

Question: What is it for The Trump White House to lie? America, remember the story of Chicken Little who was always telling people "the sky is falling, the sky is falling." And, one day, Chicken Little went out and the sky was falling, but no one would listen to him. America, understand well, and heed the unadulterated Word of God, because Jesus said it best: "Yea rather, blessed are they that hear the word of God, and keep it" (Luke 11:28). God has warned us concerning individuals such as President Donald J. Trump: "When he speaketh fair, believe him not: for there are seven abominations in his heart. Who hatred is covered by deceit, his wickedness shall be shewed before the whole congregation (nation/world)" (Proverbs 26:25-26). President Trump is a fake leader with no shame in his political game, only an insatiable desire to blame others for his own failures. Question: Whatever happened to "I and I alone can fix it"?

Blaming previous Presidential Administrations and ungodly political posturing is not public policy decision-making.

Christian Evangelicals are seemingly more spiritually in tune with SIN than the righteousness of God simply because of their overwhelming support for an individual such as President Donald J. Trump. America, this is indeed a mind-boggling, spiritually disturbing reality. Saying "Lord, Lord" and running with the devil is truly an ungodly abomination. The Christian church should never become a country club whereby pastoral leaders espouse spiritual words of inspiration from pulpits that simply fall upon deaf ears in the pews. Now, we know why Sunday morning is the most segregated hour in American society. Shame, shame, because money is the name of the game, and now we know, what "In God We Trust" truly means to Christian Evangelicals. Christian Evangelicals, understand this: "For the love of money is the root of all evil: which while some coveted after, they have erred from the faith, and pierced themselves through with many sorrows" (1 Timothy 6:10). But, nevertheless Christian Evangelicals, "God judgeth the righteous, and God is angry with the wicked every day" (Psalms 7:11).

Christians should never support ungodly leadership mentalities such as that of President Trump and his counterpart Russian Dictator Putin, especially with nuclear capacity at their finger-tips. God has declared no more water, but the fire next time. Moreover, God has given us the privilege of self-governance—the sacred, democratic right to vote. And, if individuals do not intelligently know what to vote for, just maybe they should stay home. By the way, not voting is not a godly choice, but it is probably more desirable than placing an ungodly individual in The White House (The Peoples' House).

America, has experienced 100 days of hell because, we have a spiritually misguided President who does not understand democratic-leadership, but has an ungodly love for communistic dictatorship. President Trump, for the past 100 days, has been acting as though he is stuck on hellish stupidity. As a result, American society has experienced hell and is spiritually upside down without positive solutions to any of its socio-economic-problems. American society is in socio-political turmoil: its democratic institutions are being compromised, and an ungodly war is on the horizon in order to protect against impending impeachment proceedings for treason. Moreover, making off-the-wall war talk, and sword-rattling, against an unstable, dictatorial regime together produce a recipe for world annihilation. We all know that a war-time President will not be impeached or lose a Presidential election. America, remember what God told Samuel (Israel's last judge) to tell the Israelites about their desire for a king, as well as their desire to be like other nations: "And the Lord said unto Samuel, Hearken unto the voice of the people in all that they say unto thee: for they have not rejected thee, but they have rejected me, that I should not reign over them…And Samuel heard all of the words of the people, and he rehearsed them in the ears of the Lord. And the Lord said to Samuel, Hearken unto their voice: howbeit yet protest solemnly unto them, and shew them the manner of the King that shall reign over them" (1 Samuel 8:6-9). God warned the Israelites: A King can be compromised; but the Israelites could not compromise the man of God (Samuel). And, of course, Saul was not God's choice for King of the Israelites. On the 99th day of his Presidency, Donald J. Trump told the world in so many words: "I was qualified to be President (American Citizen), but I was not ready to be President of a Great Nation. Because I did not know the complexity of American social democracy and the amount of complicated work involved." Once again, what ever happened to "I and I alone can fix it"? It's not easy being the President of the greatest nation on the planet.

Unfortunately, the Republican Party has become a nationalistic (White Privilege-oriented) Grievance Party, that is, a Political Party whose voting-base is made-up of individuals who have socio-economic grievances against our democratic system of government based upon race/ethnicity as The Angry White Privilege Right, not The Christian Evangelical Right. Base-line Republican voters are using socio-economic issues simply as a way to mask racism, bigotry, and sexism. The Party of Lincoln is spiritually dead. The Southern Dixiecrat Party and the Party of Reagan is alive and well, but the Party of Lincoln (Grand Ole Party) is dead. To top it off, we have had disastrous Republican Town Hall Meetings that turned into shouting matches and mayhem, the legislative debacle of repeal and replace Obamacare, building a Mexican-Style/Berlin-Style Wall, the General Flynn Treason Investigation, Presidential midnight tweeting, The Trump-style War brigade, and the North Korean Mad Man Show. Question: Three more years of this? God help us all, even though God has already blessed America. But, too many Americans refuse to bless and honor God! America, we are on the edge of midnight; and God is angry with the wicked everyday as well as those who seek to perpetuate evil. Thus: "Let us therefore come boldly unto the throne of grace, that we may obtain mercy, and find grace to help in time of need" (Hebrews 4:16). Amen! Amen! Amen!

THE MISSING LINK: FATHERLESS TRAINING

Marriage is of God. Therefore, the criteria for a godly marriage, since marriage is of God, are that both the man and the woman should be a born again Christian, that is "equally yoked." "Believe on the Lord Jesus Christ, and thou shalt be saved, and thy house" (Acts 16:31). Men (husbands and fathers), if no one has ever told you this spiritual truth, please allow me to inform you: marriage is a total commitment, not a part-time sexual affair. Most marriages fail because of the love of money, sexual issues, and substance abuse addictions. "Marriage is honourable in all, and the bed is undefiled: but whoremongers and adulterers God will judge" (Hebrews 13:4). Christian men, regardless of socio-economic circumstances (jobs or no jobs), family obligations are spiritually greater, because God plus you equals success in any endeavor. Hence, "Likewise, ye husbands, dwell with them according to knowledge, giving honour unto the wife, as unto the weaker vessel, and as being heirs together of the grace of life; that your prayers be not hindered" (1 Peter 3:7).

God has family on his mind and so should every God-fearing individual. As a matter of fact, lest we forget, God is the designer of family, not the U.S. Supreme Court. Joshua said it best: "And if it seem evil unto you to serve the Lord, choose you this day whom ye will serve; whether the gods which your fathers served that were on the other side of the flood, or the gods of the Amorites, in whose land ye dwell: but as for me and my house, we will serve the Lord" (Joshua 24:15). Salvation comes through the generations. After all, this is why the New Testament Gospel begins with the genealogy of Jesus to establish that He is the descendant of both King David and Abraham, just as the Old Testament had predicted.

Society begins and ends in family units, and when family units become dysfunctional, society begins to decline. The spiritual-moral walls begin to crumble. Prior to 1965, the overwhelming majority of America's children grew up in two-parent families. Today, the reverse is true. The question is: why does this spiritual moral state of being exist in twenty-first century America? Why has American society been able to create sophisticated robots (machines) and guided missiles, and, at the same time, spiritually misguided individuals? The answer lies in the breakdown of family in American culture. Men, we are much better than what currently exists in American culture, and therefore, we must become more spiritual through faith and through becoming Christ-like. God has already solemnly declared, "Whoso findeth a wife (woman) findeth a good thing, and obtaineth favour of the Lord" (Proverbs 18:22).

The importance of spiritual-social roles in family structures as well as societal importance cannot be understated. God designed the family based upon men and women playing different (specific), but equally important socio-spiritual roles. Mothers are to be the teachers of love within family units, especially love for fathers. Fathers are to be the Godly trainers within family structures who are to train children in the "way of the Lord" (God's principles and precepts), not the way of the vanity of the world. Family is the first school. Scripturally, the role of the father is to: "Train up a child in the way he should go: and when he is old, he will not depart from it" (Proverbs 22: 6). Children are being mis-educated by parents in their homes as well as mis-educated by professional educators in public school systems. Mis-education is primarily mis-education in the Word of God. This is why the Bible declares, "If ye continue in my word, then are ye my disciples indeed; and ye shall know the truth, and the truth shall make you free" (John 8:31-32). Make you free from what? Man's social doctrine of confusion about himself rather than God's spiritual doctrine about who he is, as expressed in the life and teachings of our Lord and Savior Jesus Christ, the Righteous One. "Professing themselves to be wise, they became fools, and changed the glory of the uncorruptible God into an image made like to corruptible man…" (Romans 1:22-23).

Here's the question of questions: Why did the founders finesse the separation of church and state? The answer lies in the social sources of denominationalism. We need God in our educational processes because God has emphatically stated, "Blessed is he that readeth, and they that hear the words of this prophecy, and keep those things which are written therein" (Revelation 1:3). Education in the "way of the Lord" is the only lasting, eternal way to internalize a spiritual relationship with God since life is about journey to meet God. Of course, this is why, we must: "Seek ye first the kingdom of God, and his righteousness; and all these things shall be added unto you" (Matthew 6:33). More importantly, "As it is appointed unto men once to die, but after this the judgment" (Hebrews 9:27). Let everyone be perfectly clear that "God judgeth the righteous, and God is angry with the wicked every day" (Psalm 7:11).

All of us should remember the inspirational words of Whitney Houston: "Children are our future." Men, children are your immortal legacy (seed). Why do you leave your children high and dry on a creek, in a boat, without oars, flowing with the current in dangerous waters? The time has come for you to be men of God by accepting your responsibilities as heads of household and leading your families to the Promised Land. This sounds hard, but it is just as hard doing wrong-headed things knowing full well that you ultimately face eternal judgment.

Christian Evangelicals are so caught up in the vanity-flesh orientation of material empire building and naming-and-claiming rather than acknowledging JESUS in all of his glory. This is why American society is caught-up in a death-wish with an ungodly President who is hell-bent on leading American society into a place of no return—a nuclear holocaust. Elections have consequences; and most assuredly, Trump Voters, you wanted a "Great White Hope" but have received a Great White Fool instead. Now, America is the ugly America, and the laughing-stock of the free world with our democratic allies completely confused, wondering "what in the hell is going on?" America, there is no godly wisdom, governmental-intellectual understanding, or moral conscience in President Trump's Administration. Godly fathers, wake-up and reclaim your children's heritage from vanity. Selah!

An Analysis of the Political Party System in America

Politics in American society has denigrated into an ungodly partisan power struggle, rather than universal governance oriented toward maximizing the common good. This unfortunate set of circumstances is due to the super-rich instituting a zero sum economic game: the super-rich win and the American people lose. What is fueling this socio-political-economic approach is the fact that one political party is married to this super-rich philosophical approach and the other political party is engaged to be married. In the final analysis, the Corporate Party wins and the American people lose. Presently, in American society, roughly two percent of the population received over seventy percent of the nation's increase in wealth since the economic recovery of 2008. Economically, over fifty percent of the American population cannot come up with two thousand dollars in thirty days. Women only earn seventy-seven cents for every dollar men earn; and, at the same time, in the majority of households in America, women are the primary wage earners. These facts suggest that many white voters, especially white males, vote against their own best economic interests. The question is: why?

Both political parties are committing societal adultery, because greed is greed and there are no degrees of greed. This set of political circumstances has created a dysfunctional major political party system: Republican Party and Democratic Party. Currently, both major political parties have their moral-political shortcomings. And, of course, the spiritual principles of social democracy suffer because of political confusion. Both major political parties, to varying degrees, are guilty of dividing America in the worst kind of way: dividing families and dividing the rich from the poor. It has rightly been said, "If you did it unto the least of them, you did it unto me."

Initially, the Republican Party was based upon sound doctrinal governing principles and a common sense, big-tent approach to governance. As time passed, because of the Civil Rights Act of 1964 and the Voting Rights Act of 1965, the Republican Party began to embrace the Southern Dixie-Crat political philosophy concerning power, economic advantage, and political electability. And, of course, the seed-bed for this political approach was the Goldwater limited government strategy which culminated in Reaganomics. Couple the John Birch Society with Reaganomics and this philosophy made many rural and suburban dwellers feel as though Minorities were getting something for nothing. This is primarily the case because the Republican Party has become primarily a Southern Regional Party. Sadly, the Republican Party is functioning upon a political model that is obsolete. Additionally, President Reagan coined politically emotional phrases to galvanize independent voters, rural and suburban dwellers: "welfare queen," "give-away social programs," and "law and order." Unfortunately, the current two-party political system has polarized American society and, at the same time, created social class prejudice rather than societal spiritual unity. In fact, major political parties have so polarized politics and governance in American society that many Americans now define themselves as "independents," that is in the middle of nothingness. Sadly, too many politicians are concerned with the next election rather than the next generation. Instead of planning to plant trees they are cutting down trees. Unlike the Republican Party, the Democratic Party has a big tent progressive political philosophy and, therefore, can absorb more readily different kinds of political philosophies/factions. To be sure, sometimes this philosophical political approach creates unbridled factionalism as well.

The Tea Party is an ultra-cultural conservative exclusionary faction of the Republican Party. Seemingly, the primary objective is to hang on the front-door of the Republican Party a subliminal message: whites only, no minorities wanted. These types of signs physically existed prior to the 1964 Civil Rights Act and the Voting Rights Act of 1965. Living in the past is not a healthy political strategy nor is this approach a sound societal spiritual unity strategy, because the past was not perfect. It belongs to the devil and the future belongs to God. The present moment belongs to individuals. The Tea Party appears to be anti-fairness and therefore more interested in acquiring economic privileges rather than equitable political governance inclusion. On the other hand, the Republican Party has positioned itself as anti-minority and the voting numbers tend to bear out this socio-political analysis. Every individual votes in his/her own best self-interest and therefore identifies with the political party that advocates their best interest. It appears as though Democratic Party policies are in the best interest of minorities, the nation, as well as the international community. In the past, Republican Party policies were in the best interests of minorities, the nation, and the international community. Seemingly, our European allies are more in agreement with America's current diplomatic approach to international problem solving than the Republican Party, whose approach to resolving international issues appears to be militarism. America should never give comfort to or aid her foes: foreign or domestic.

The Minority Party, because of the hi-jacking of the Republican Party by the Tea Party, has been politically forced into almost wholly aligning itself with the Democratic Party. This, in and of itself, is spiritually, politically, and economically unhealthy for the well-being of the nation. The Minority Party must always be inclusive. Jesus was about inclusion because all have sinned and come short of the glory of God.

All political parties should be inclusive, that is should be of the people, by the people and for the people. Without a doubt, power for the sake of power is intellectual insanity. In order to have societal unity and world peace there must be godly, spiritual purposes associated with the exercise of power. The earth is the Lord's and the fullness thereof "and it is appointed unto men once to die, but after this the judgment" (Hebrews 9:27). Godly men and women understand this universal power principle. Therefore, when individuals are faithful over a few things, they will know how to rule (exercise power) over many things. God has spoken to every generation and His message (theology) from one generation to the next has not changed. Even in the twenty-first century God is still changing deserts into green pastures and vice versa. Therefore, all that we say and do should glorify God and, above all, be designed to love and serve each other in the spirit of unity of national purpose and, above all, world peace.

What Legacy?

These are times in which men in leadership positions refuse to listen to and live by sound doctrine. It appears that the majority of our political leaders at every level of government are desirous of taking right and making it wrong, and wrong and making it right, and making it work. "There is a way which seemeth right unto a man; but the end thereof are the ways of death" (Proverbs 14:12). Of course, we understand that "fools make a mock at sin: but among the righteous there is favor" (Proverbs 14:9). In the twenty-first century, for understandable spiritual and political reasons, things are not done decently and in order in our governmental system. Therefore, Congressional approval rating is approaching a single-digit figure, because of political governing confusion and political party discord. Unfortunately, most of the governing confusion and societal discord is caused by one political party in particular, because of the personage of the president.

All of this confusion is charged to our children as well as the next generation. Children are a gift from God. Question: what is the heritage that's being passed on to our children? Seemingly, the answer is confusion, confusion, and more confusion. Question: Does America know what God requires of her? "He hath showed thee, O man, what is good: and what doth the Lord require of thee, but to do justly, and to love mercy, and to walk humbly with thy God?" (Micah 6:8). Let's be clear: "Do not be deceived, God is not mocked: for whatever a man sows, this he will also reap" (Galatians 6:7). (If an individual or political party sows discord, they shall reap discord.) Individuals cannot have peace where there is no moral order. Above all, individuals cannot have society and civilization when individuals do not have a conscience.

The press in these United States of America should not slant news events one way or the other. There is Good News and the good news is simply this: "The Lord gave the Word: great was the company of those that published it" (Psalm 68:11). The local and national press should thoroughly research issues, and tell the American people the unadulterated truth. Slanting news events and issues create confusion, social conflict and societal discord, and above all racial/ethnic tensions. All of us should remember the solemn words of Rodney King: "Can't we all just get along?"

Every American desires to have a good name because the Bible profoundly declares, "A good name is rather to be chosen than great riches, and loving favor rather than silver or gold" (Proverbs 22:1). And, of course, President Obama is not an exception to the rule. President Obama's desire is to do well, while he can, for as many as he can, and above all how he can. President Obama understands: "Every word of God is pure: he is a shield unto them that put their trust in him" (Proverbs 30:5) But, LEGACY is the way the news media portrays Obama's presidency. Most Americans only know the legacy of a few presidents of these United States.

The poet/dramatist William Shakespeare wrote five great tragedies. In one of his great tragedies, Julius Caesar, Shakespeare analyzes Mark Antony's speech. The following quote from Mark Antony's speech lines up with every American president's term of office: "The evil that men do lives after them; The good is oft interred with their bones." So let it be with Barack Obama. The objective in this editorial is to set the record straight on President Obama's leadership accomplishments, not his legacy. The items listed below are not legacies but are social realities (truths) that have helped many Americans weather one of the worst economic down-turns in America's history. Legacy is an individual accomplishment. We all know that President Obama does not work in a vacuum. Even though the buck stops at the president's desk there is no "I" in team. Obama's administrative team is made-up of many, many dedicated hard working professionals who have accomplished the following:

- Affordable Healthcare Act (Obamacare).
- Saved the banking and automobile industries from total collapse.
- Brought Bin Laden to justice.
- The Lilly Ledbetter Fair Pay Act (equal pay for women).
- Led the economy through the worst economic crisis since The Great Depression.

The march for full citizenship for Black Americans has been marred with numerous difficult institutional obstacles. In 2015, there are too many Blacks losing their spiritual relationship with God and a leadership vision for a just society, because of the breakdown of the nuclear family structure (moral decadence). Too many Americans have become idle-minded passengers on a bus that is headed over the moral bankruptcy cliff. The moral walls have been torn down in twenty-first century America. "God standeth in the congregation of the mighty; he judgeth among the gods. How long will ye judge unjustly, and accept the persons of the wicked? Defend the poor and needy: rid them out of the hand of the wicked. They know not, neither will they understand; they walk on in darkness: all the foundations of the earth are out of course" (Psalms 82:1-5).

Lust causes individuals to love that which they should hate. "But, beloved, remember ye the words which were spoken before of the apostles of our Lord Jesus Christ; how that they told you there should be mockers in the last time, who should walk after their own ungodly lusts. These be they who separate themselves, sensual, having not the Spirit." (Jude 1:17-19). In conclusion: "Be not deceived: evil communication corrupt good manners. Awake to righteousness, and sin not; for some have not the knowledge of God: I speak this to your shame" (1 Corinthians 15:33-35).

What will your life's work say about the glory of God, a future for your children, and, above all, abundant possibilities for future generations? Selah!

A Socio-Theological Analysis of Vanity

Why are so many Americans in an uproar and so many more Americans devising vain things? To a large degree, the answer lies in the feminizing of American culture, the mass media communications-entertainment industry, and the lustful greed for money. When you get right down to it, instant gratification is at the crux of the problem.

The wisest man who ever lived said it best: "All is vanity" (Ecclesiastes 3:18-22). Chasing after pleasure is dangerous to your spiritual well-being. God gives every individual a spiritual test, and the test results are in: "There is no advantage of men over beasts. They have the same breathe and both die." "Professing themselves to be wise, they became fools" (Romans 1:22). When you think you know more than God, you are indeed a fool. The real question is: "Where were you when the foundations of the earth were formed?"

Therefore, "Fools make a mock at sin: but among the righteous there is favor" (Proverbs 14:9). Sin is not a civil rights issue. Sin is a spiritual and moral issue. But some men who think themselves to be wise, but who are foolish in the sight of God, have made sin a governmental civil rights issue. But God does not make mistakes. There is a time and place for all things under the sun. In short, there is a right time and a right place for everything. But some even say that there is a right way to do wrong. "For all have sinned, and come short of the glory of God" (Romans 3:23). From this declaration, let me take you to a higher level of transfiguration: "Therefore, being justified by faith, we have peace with God through our Lord Jesus Christ: by whom also we have access by faith into this grace wherein we stand, and rejoice in hope of the Glory of God" (Romans 5:1). Knowing the difference and seizing the moment is the key. In short, an individual cannot sleep walk through life.

A visionary leadership mentality is the foundation of every society. George Washington had such a mentality. Abraham Lincoln had such a mentality. Franklin D. Roosevelt had such a mentality. Therefore, when the leadership foundation is corrupted, society perishes. "Except the Lord of hosts had left unto us a very small remnant we would have been as Sodom and we would have been like unto Gomorrah" (Isaiah 1:9). God left a remnant of a "few good men" to guide and direct them through trying/perilous times.

It is definitely not the Republicans, because they have become too negative. And of course it is not the Democrats, because they have become too progressive. God is not a God of conservative cultural negativity, and He is definitely not a God of progressive feminized vanity. "For those who guide this people are leading them astray; and those who are guided by them are brought to confusion" (Isaiah 9:16). For it is written, "Whosoever believes that Jesus is the Christ is born of God, and whoever loves the Father loves the child born of Him" (1 John 5:1). For after all, God is life.

The breakdown of family life (into single-parent households) and the moral failure of the Christian church and its unbridled monetary orientation for materialism (church buildings) rather than spiritualism (community development), is what is fueling the flames of immoral fleshly vanity. Couple cultural Christianity with "stand your ground" laws born out of "ethnic" fear (which invariably makes cowards of us all), and what we have is mass societal confusion. The principle of unwarranted fear is what is motivating such laws. Enforcement of such laws is always the problem—not necessarily the laws.

The feminizing of America is born out of an over-materialistic, vanity-centered perspective on life, simply because it has become easier for some men to become passive rather than standing up like God-fearing men. This passivity, or feminization, does not necessarily mean homosexuality. This phenomenon exists because too many illegitimate parents are placing their pleasure-principle vanity needs above their parental responsibility and the developmental needs of their children. Of course, what is operating behind the matriarchal society scene in which we live is that it is easier for females, especially minority females, to become meaningfully/gainfully employed. This is a central contributing factor to the feminization of America, and of course this economic set of circumstances is fueling spiritual and social conflict between men and women.

As the sole providers of their families' basic material/survival needs, too many single mothers are teaching their male children to love their mothers and hate their fathers. Children are very impressionable and they learn through imitation. Therefore, adults should be careful of the examples they set. Female children are taught by their mothers, "Don't depend on a man: get an education"; and, of course, male children get caught-up in the same social vortex. This is not the full picture of the feminizing of American culture, only a snap-shot view. The operative expression used by many women is, "I can do bad by myself."

Too much enmity exists between men and women, and institutional Christianity is not helping to foster the spiritual and moral principle that America was founded on—"In God We Trust." If men and women do not trust God and the Word of God, there is no way that they can trust each other. Without a doubt, the prison system is designed to feminize men. Of course, the question is: Who is in prison?

Society begins and ends in the family, and when family structure disintegrates, society becomes spiritually and morally bankrupt, because there is no spiritual-moral structure informing what we think, say, or do. To alleviate the negative consequences of an instant gratification, vanity-oriented American society, the family structure, the church, and educational institutions must be spiritual and morally revamped. One "side" does not fit all. Centralized bureaucratic madness is not working. We need to change the centralized madness in our educational systems to holistic community-oriented education; that is the holistic educational development of family, church, and school. This is the only way we can overcome the conditions of social vanity that are eroding the spiritual foundation of American society. The overriding issue is moral and spiritual integration, not ethnic/racial integration, because no society can exist unless individuals have a moral conscience. When individuals have moral peace with God, they have societal peace with each other. So be it.

Life is About Priorities

Life is about priorities. A priority is a value-ordering of one's life. Values dictate institutional structures, as well as family lifestyles. Learning how to order one's personal and family lifestyle in terms of knowledge and understanding where to place one's ultimate trust is of primary importance. Vanity is spiritually dangerous, because vanity creates debt. And, debt is a form of slavery. This is precisely why the Bible declares: "Owe no man anything, but to love one another: for he that loveth another hath fulfilled the law" (Romans 13:8). LOVE fulfills God's requirements. "Drinking the vanity of the world and not thinking is a bad combination, because life is ultimately about making mistakes.

Every individual makes mistakes, but it is not the mistakes that individuals make, but it is the inability of individuals to change, that is, to learn to live in spite of their mistakes. Doing the same thing over and over is the classic definition of insanity according to the world. Real change comes from having societal knowledge, spiritual knowledge, and a personal relationship with God. "If we say that we have fellowship with him, and walk in darkness, we lie, and do not the truth: but if we walk in the light, as he is in the light, we have fellowship one with another, and the blood of Jesus Christ his Son cleanseth us from all sin" (1 John 1:6-7).

Let's be clear about this particular scripture, because this scripture does not mean entitlement to salvation and being born again. It is only the first step in the process of salvation. For every individual must experience sanctification: "Sanctify them through thy truth: thy word is truth. As thou hast sent me into the world, even so have I also sent them into the world. And for their sakes I sanctify myself, that they also might be sanctified through the truth" (John 17:17-19). Every individual must understand the process of receiving salvation, and therefore, understand this scripture, because all of us sin either through omission or commission: "But grow in grace, and in the knowledge of our Lord and Savior Jesus Christ. To him be glory both now and forever. Amen" (2 Peter 3:18). Therefore, every individual must acknowledge this reference: "Verily, verily I say unto thee, Except a man be born again, he cannot see the Kingdom of God" (John 3:5). Get off the premises and get on the promise."

Above all, spiritually understanding what are the most important things about living a meaningful, fulfilling life is the key to having a successful life rather than merely having material success in life. This is why Jesus always confronted individuals with this question: Where do you place your ultimate trust? Whom do you love the most—the Creator of the creation? Counting the spiritual cost is a very important element in living a spiritually meaningful life. This is why Jesus always urged individuals to count the cost: "Take heed, and beware of covetousness: for a man's life consisteth not in the abundance of the things which he possesseth" (Luke 12:15).

Living life from the outside in does not afford an individual the possibility of developing an internal values system which is based upon intellectual integrity, moral character, and spiritual understanding. Unfortunately, Christian leadership has encouraged the valuing of tangibles (things) rather than intangibles (moral character, intellectual integrity, and spiritual understanding). On Sunday, October 23, 2016 in Sumter, South Carolina, at the St. Paul AME ? Church one parishioner violently stabbed another parishioner during worship services. In the twenty-first century, individuals cannot attend church and worship God in Spirit and Truth without being subject to potentially losing one's life. Question: "How shall we escape, if we neglect so great salvation; which at first began to be spoken by the Lord, and was confirmed unto us by them that heard him..." (Hebrews 2:3). For we all know that "for with the heart man believeth unto righteousness; and with the mouth confession is made unto salvation." (Romans 10:10).

The challenges of creative living in a spiritually dying culture of having or not having the material creature comforts of the American Dream are much easier to face when individuals have their spiritual life-styles in order. The missing moral links in the family structure and Christian leadership mentalities are the sources of the problems destroying American culture. Culture is not GOD. Even though, religion and culture can invariably become one.

Society begins and ends in family structure, and when the family structure deteriorates society declines spiritually and morally. To be sure, in twenty-first century, American families are recycling dysfunctional spiritual curses from generation to generation. Family relationships are the foundation for moral character development. Life is about character development. The David and Saul saga was about moral character development. King Saul had been hunting David to kill him. David could have killed King Saul, but he rose above the code of "an eye for an eye and a tooth for a tooth." When Saul finally met David face to face, he saw himself for what he really was and he broke down, lifted up his voice and wept. "Thou art more righteous than I, for thou hast rewarded me good, whereas I have rewarded thee evil" (Samuel 24:17). Great is the individual that rules his own Spirit (mind), because greater is he that rules his own spirit than he who takes a city.

Character development is about spiritual and internal values, and the valuing of people rather than valuing things and the pleasure-principle. American society is in dire need of the spiritual-moral integration of flesh and SPIRIT. But, just like Pilate, too many Americans have washed their hands in despair, called it quits, and said let the record stand. Yes, we may always have institutional racism, sexism, classism and socio-economic injustice, because there will always be those who are not willing to set positive moral examples of character and intellectual integrity for others to imitate. America, "We are troubled on every side, yet not distressed; we are perplexed, but not in despair; persecuted but not forsaken; cast down, but not destroyed" (2 Corinthians 4:8-9). Selah!

The Issue of Sin is Destroying the Fabric of American Society

"Wherefore, as by one man sin entered into the world, and death by sin; and so death passed upon all men, for all have sinned" (Romans 5:12). In all of our spiritual teachings we acknowledge that we render unto Caesar that which belongs to Caesar and we render unto God that which belongs to God, because all good and perfect gifts come from God. Legalizing and commercializing sin is not an effective godly strategy for dealing with sin, especially for a society whose Constitution is biblically/spiritually grounded. Nor can you solve the problem of sin with guns and bombs. Only love and the practice of love overcome sin. The problem of sin comes from a moral separation from God, both individual and societal. A saint is a sinner saved by God's grace and mercy through the birth, teachings, death, resurrection, and ascension of Jesus Christ. "For whatsoever is born of God overcometh the world, even our faith. Who is he that overcometh the world, but he that believeth that Jesus is the Son of God?" (1 John 5:4-5). Based upon the rampant nature of sin that now characterizes American culture, America is truly in need of a rebirth of the human spirit. "For he hath made him to be sin for us, who knew no sin; that we might be made the righteousness of God in him" (2 Corinthians 5:21).

Again, sin is moral separation from the reality of God (ultimate truth). All human beings sin and fall short of the glory and expectations of God. There is no such animal as a little sin or big sin. Sin is sin. However, if individuals commit the same sin over and over again, then God gives them over to a reprobate mind (Romans 1:28-32).

In analyzing the term "human being," we can readily discern that the word "human" is a compound word. "Hu" comes from the word "humus" or dirt. As humans, our bodies were made from dirt. "Man" refers to mind. It is in the mind where our souls are housed. God gives each individual a mind with free will that is, the freedom of choice. No individual can take free will choice away from another individual. Finally, the concept of "being" is ontological in nature (i.e., spiritual). Yet we are becoming materialists rather than spiritualists.

Human sexuality is the most private of all human activities. Sexuality should be closed-door business between consenting adults in the manner in which God ordained. In other words, human sexuality is not a civil right; it is private and personal business. I must vehemently confess: "Lay hands suddenly on no man, neither be partaker of other men's sins: keep thyself pure" (1Timothy 5:21). Every individual has his/her own personal sin (cross to bear); therefore we should not help another person to sin. Instead, we should always bring to the attention of others that the wages of sin is death, but the gift of God is eternal life through Jesus Christ our Lord and Savior (Romans 6:23). The Holy Bible is the only standard for judging what sin is. God commands that we love one another, because He loves us so much that He gave his only begotten Son for our soul salvation (John 3:16). This is why we must always disapprove of sin. "Love the sinner and have hatred for the sin, because sin is of the devil."

Without a doubt, an "A" is an "A", just as a "V" is a "V". They have different sounds phonetically as well as different functions in the alphabetical system. On the one hand, taking an "A" and flipping it upside down and removing the crossbar in no way alter the phonetic functional sound that is its purpose. An "A" is still an "A" and a "V" is still a "V". On the other hand, taking the "Cross" out of human affairs alters everything. For after all, the "Cross" is about individual/collective responsibility. God and nature ordained the "V" body part to be the vehicle for birthing life. The "A" body part is the vehicle for death excretion. Exchanging body part processes in order to maximize the pleasure principle in no way alters the divine/natural purpose.

A clarion call has been issued. The opportunity has come. The question is: what shall we do with the country that God has tremendously blessed to be the spiritual/moral light of the world? America's internal morality cannot be based upon an "each to his own way" philosophy. When you get right down to it, human self-centeredness fosters spiritual/moral bankruptcy. The federal government does far more good than bad; therefore Americans should insist with godly fervor that the government not legalize sin. American culture has become too materialistic and paganistic. Indeed, America is on the brink of a spiritual and moral collapse into chaos. When God-fearing Americans see the writing on the wall we need to declare that enough is enough. God gave Noah the rainbow sign: no more water, but the fire next time. Sodom and Gomorrah serve as a classic example of the judgment of Almighty God. So be it.

Sin is Not a Civil Rights Issue

The U.S. Constitution declares that all individuals have the God-given right based upon free will to pursue happiness. There is individual free will, and at the same time, there is God's commandment against sin. "And as it is appointed unto men once to die, but after this the judgment" (Hebrews 9:27). Let's not fool ourselves. "God judgeth the righteous, and God is angry with the wicked every day" (Psalms 7:11).

The scenario for human sexuality has been established by God Almighty in the HOLY BIBLE. Sexuality purely for vain pleasure is sin whether it is heterosexuality in nature or homosexuality in nature. Sexuality is private business, not public opinion or public policy. What goes on behind closed doors between consenting adults is between those adults and God. Once again, "God judgeth the righteous, and God is angry with the wicked every day" (Hebrews 9: 27). Make no mistake about it: "Jesus Christ the same yesterday, and today, and forever." (Hebrews 13:8). And, believe the BIBLE, Jesus is not about to change for any sinner, because the Gospel is designed to change the sinner, and not the sinner to change the Gospel. However, He (Jesus) will forgive all sinners if they ask forgiveness, and repent of their sins, because "Forever, O Lord thy word is settled in heaven" (Psalms 119:89).

Know this: "There is no wisdom nor understanding nor counsel against the Lord" (Proverbs 21:30). Before we proceed to a conclusion, let's be absolutely clear about the word of God: "But she (he) that liveth in pleasure is dead while she (he) liveth" (1 Timothy 5:6). All sins are against the spiritual commandments of God: "Be fruitful, and multiply, and replenish the earth, and subdue it" (Genesis 1:28).

Sin is a God issue; not an issue of civil rights, because sin is about free will choices. Individuals have a decision (say), but in the final analysis of all things, God has the last word. Individuals are born with goodness, and of course, family and communal environments must nurture spirituality and goodness, not carnal mindedness.

Same-sex sexuality is a covenant with spiritual and physical death, and in the end same-sex sexuality creates a physical culture of death. Two males cannot fulfill God's spiritual command, and neither can two females. Glorifying death in either its real or symbolic dimension (form) is an unwise proposition. Life is not about death. Life is about creative spiritual living. Spiritual obedience to God is greater than sacrifice, especially when individuals are seeking the truth. The biological truth is simply this: Life does not come through same-sex sexuality. Therefore, do not become a lifetime card-carrying member of the walking dead club.

Physical death is inevitable. Individuals have no choice whatsoever in the matter. Even suicide is not a real choice. Why kill yourself? Just wait on God; keep on living, and physical death will come knocking on your door. Just be ready to go, and even if you are not ready to go, you are going to go any way!

Human beings are the only form of animal life that can engage in sexuality both for procreation, as well as recreation (pleasure). Lower forms of animal life are programmed by God and nature to engage in sexuality only when they can reproduce their specie. This is why, we all should know, that sexuality in the human experience is all about choice. Without a doubt, individuals cannot satisfy vanity; it's of the devil, and the devil deals in death (spiritual and physical). The devil wants you dead one way or the other.

Above all, know this: "Mortify therefore your members which are upon the earth; fornication, uncleanness, inordinate affection (homosexuality, incest, bestiality), evil concupiscence, and covetousness, which is idolatry: for which things' sake the wrath of God cometh on the children of disobedience: in which ye also walked sometime, when he lived in them" (Colossians 3:5-7). God desires that we consider ourselves unresponsive and dead to evil desires and influences of the devil. This is why God warns us against sexual perversion. The Bible celebrates heterosexuality and marriage as the proper relationship for sexual fulfillment, because sexual perversion will turn the heart of your mind away from God and toward vanity and the influences of the devil. Individuals cannot make right wrong and wrong right. This will not fly in the face of God. To God be the glory in Jesus's name! Amen! Amen! Amen!

WHY HAS THE BATHROOM BECOME AN ISSUE OF CIVIL RIGHTS?

American society is devolving into absolute spiritual and moral chaos. As Americans, we continually look back at sin because there are monetary benefits in sinning. If there weren't, individuals would not sin. Of course, this is precisely why, in the state of North Carolina, the conversation concerning the bathroom is about monetary loses and political "B.S.," not spirituality or morality. However, it is recorded: "For the love of money is the root of all evil: which some coveted after, they have erred from the faith, and pierced themselves through with many sorrows" (1 Timothy 6:10). God told Lot and his family "don't look back" at sin! In fact, the spiritual-moral decadence over the so-called issue of gender identity concerning bathroom facilities is a glaring example of "looking back" at sin (Genesis 19:1-26). The bathroom is a biological, functionary, excretion issue, not an issue of Civil Rights or gender equality. Why, then, has the bathroom in the twenty-first century been elevated as an issue of gender equality and Civil Rights? In other words, why have urine and feces become an issue of Civil Rights rather than biological functions?

In the Bible, it is recorded that King Solomon was the wisest man to have lived simply because he asked God for wisdom in order to lead others by example. King Solomon did not ask God for money (wealth). But, God gave Solomon enormous wealth because he asked God for the right thing. By the way, a positive example is the greatest teacher. Without a doubt, America is setting some ungodly examples for its children as well as future generations. King Solomon declared: "I am black, but comely, O ye daughters of Jerusalem, as the tents of Kedar, as the curtains of Solomon. Look not upon me, because I am black, because the sun hath looked upon me" (Song of Solomon 1:5-6). Question: Is it logical that one bright and glorious morning King Solomon would awaken and boldly declare that he was White and no longer Black? Especially since his blackness was a part of his biological identity (DNA)! America, hear me well! God does not make mistakes because God is perfect in righteousness and "righteousness exalteth a nation: but sin is a reproach to any people" (Proverbs 14:34). For after all, it is sin which causes all human beings to be imperfect, but we must strive for perfection in doing the Will of God (Two Great Commandments): "Thou shalt love the Lord thy God with all thy heart, and with all thy soul, and with all thy mind. And this is the first and greatest commandment. And the second is like unto it, Thou shalt love thy neighbor as thyself. On these two commandments hang all the law and the prophets" (Matthew 22:37-40).

Sin produces vanity. Vanity fosters lust of the flesh. As a matter of fact, what is vanity to one individual is reality to another. Unfortunately, in some individuals, reality and vanity form a marriage of confusion, and these individuals then live in a delusional state of being. Remember Christians: "God is not the author of confusion, but of peace, as in all churches of the saints" (1 Corinthians 14:33).

Individuals confuse themselves with their own ungodly interpretations and imaginations; and, thus, God has told us to interpret the "Word of God" for what it is: "I am the way, the truth, and the life: no man cometh unto the father, but by me" (John 14:6). More importantly, God states emphatically: "Before I formed thee in the belly I knew thee: and before thou camest forth out of the womb I sanctified thee" (Jeremiah 1:5). Unfortunately, in some instances, parents, extended family members, environmental socialization, and peer group influences created internal confusion in some individuals. And, there are some parents who desire a female child and a male child is born, and through parental socialization they oftentimes confuse the child, but God and the doctor were not confused: they know what came forth from the mother's womb. Whatever the case may be, don't blame God; and don't be too hard on yourself either. But, through it all, always remember it is still about free-will. "For as he thinketh in his heart, so is he" (Proverbs 23:7).

The spiritual confusion that is running rampant in American society concerning public bathroom usage is directly linked to the breakdown of the nuclear family, Christian pastoral leadership, lack of Biblical expository teaching/preaching, the loss of sacredness in American Christianity, political immorality (hooking and crooking), and ungodliness in public educational institutions. This Biblical scriptural verse is absolutely revelatory, "His watchmen are blind: they are ignorant, they are all dumb dogs, they cannot bark; sleeping, lying down loving to slumber" (Isaiah 56:10). The breakdown of sacredness in American society has produced an insatiable desire for spiritually inappropriate human interpersonal relationships; even bestiality is promoted in certain sectors of American society. Public bathroom usage is not an issue of public policy. Moreover, when interpersonal relationships between God, individuals, and families spiritually-morally break down, urine and feces hit the fan, and human feces flies everywhere. Above all, life in American society has begun to stink to high heaven, and its foul smell is then sent to hell.

TO BE OR NOT TO BE IS THE QUESTION! To be what you are is the real thing. To be what you think you want to be, in fact, may be different from what God created you to be; or, in fact, what the doctor told your parents you were since he was the first one to see your anatomy. The Bathroom is designed for the elimination of waste. Eating (food) and drinking (water) sustains life. This is why Jesus said, "If you continue in my word, then are ye my disciples indeed; and ye shall know the truth, and the truth shall make you free" (John 8:31-32). TRUTH makes us free and lies enslave us to sinning. Hence, Jesus told us: "Why seek ye the living among the dead?" (Luke 24:5). Behold, America, stop looking for life, and life more abundantly in the bathroom, especially in the midst of that which is dead. The word of God is crystal clear. In Biblical times it was, "Hear, O Israel." In the twenty-first century, the Word of God is still crystal clear, "Hear, O America": "Lay hands suddenly on no man, neither be partaker of other men's sins: keep thyself pure" (1 Timothy 5:22). Sin is about motives (choices), and therefore, every individual has his/her own sin(s) that must be given an account of to God. Selah!

How to Win With a Bad Hand

Black Americans have been dealt a bad hand based upon skin color because Whites have arbitrarily made life about skin color. But, of course, Blacks spiritually know that life is about moral character and intellectual integrity, not about skin-color. Therefore, Blacks in general do not view their skin color as having been dealt a bad hand. Of course, this is why many Blacks live meaningful lives in spite of the institutional restrictions because of their skin color.

The human mind is God's most precious gift to individuals. Indeed, the mind is very delicate and even frail. Human will is also a precious gift from God. Lack of motivation, inadequate discipline, and the absence of personal integrity can do to one's mind what lack of exercise and improper eating habits can do to one's physical health. Having a worldly mind rather than a spiritual mind in a racially-oriented society just might leave you with a bad hand. Making life a continuing learning experience is largely a matter of developing the mind. Therefore, if an individual is not developing a spiritually positive mindset, he may well be creating a formidable foe: himself. After all, an individual's mind is his best defense against dehumanization and exploitation of either self or others. Character is about spiritual and internal values rather than material and external values. Life is about the choices we make. This is precisely why you can win even when you are dealt a bad hand, societally, because of skin color. Life is choice-driven. Choices have consequences: good and bad. Without a doubt, America has dealt Blacks a bad hand called: institutional racism.

- Here's the formula for how to win with a bad hand:
- Face your fears. If at first you do not succeed try, try, and try again.
- Forget your failures. Press on toward the high calling modeled in the life and teachings of Jesus Christ.
- Take ownership of your own destiny. It is not about what happens to you, but how you respond to what happens to you. Individuals cannot always control what happens, but we can control how we respond to what happens.
- It is not cool to be stupid or dumb. Success comes by making the right life choices. Success does not come to you; you must go after it (success).
- Where there is predictability, there is also stability and accountability.

It's self-assessment time in the Black community: It's house cleaning time in the Black community. The personal baggage of some of our political and pastoral leaders is getting in the way of a healthy Black community institutionally. It's church cleaning time. The church institutionally is too important to the well-being of the Black community to be dysfunctional. Institutional Christianity should be about spiritual and moral character development, not money making schemes. Question: how do we repair lives in order that church-goers might live spiritually creative/productive lives? That is, how do we share the love of God that was expressed in how Jesus lived and in the way He died? That is, how can we have heaven on earth as articulated in the Lord's Prayer? It is also political leadership accountability time in the Black community. Our political leaders sometimes forget that they were elected by the people to give the people a voice in political matters. God anoints them and allow them to become leaders in our community. They should not take their responsibilities lightly because they are accountable, not only to the people but also to God.

God is God and there is none other beside Him. His sovereignty is unquestionable. He is God and there is nothing impossible with God. With God there is no such thing as a bad hand. The question is: who is on the Lord's side? In the twenty-first century, far too many individuals in the Black community seem to be operating on the devil's side.

A perpetual question that searches the heart of man is, "Who do you want, Jesus or Barrabas?" Think before answering because Barrabas was a patriot and Jesus was the Savior! There are many patriots, but only one Savior. Black-on-Black crime has become a vulgar and shameful expression of cannibalism (i.e., internalized self-hatred). Of course, this state of affairs exists because of lack of self-discipline and institutional moral integrity.

The classic example of how to win with a bad hand is the Biblical saga between David and King Saul (1 Samuel 1-22).

Black history begins with a positive "who am I?" experience within the family context. Therefore, if your individual answer to this state of affairs is, "I am a child of God," then you can make your own history, and not become a pleasure-seeker, hero-worshipper and above all one who seeks to keep-up with the "Joneses." To be sure, all history is salvation history, that is, God seeking to give every individual life eternally. Black history should never become hero-worship. Learning to make you your best friend is the key to a successful life, rather than having material success in life. Success is not in material possessions. Individuals are born naked and leave only with a covering over their bodies.

Blacks are the most influential socio-economic group in American society and therefore we are an integral part of American society. In order for Blacks to alleviate their victimization status because of their economic position in American society, we must make spiritual changes in our homes, churches, and educational institutions. Without a doubt, Blacks need to come together with a clear spiritual understanding: "That all things must be done decently and in order"— God's order. We need spiritual unity and a renaissance in all of our basic institutions. And, at the same time, America needs divine intervention.

What Color Is Racism?

A white male caller on C-SPAN's Washington Journal asked this question: "What color is racism?" The intent of the caller was to create confusion. Racism is not necessarily about skin color (even though in America it is about skin color). Racism is about institutionalized power. That is, racism is the power ability of an individual or group of individuals, regardless of skin color, to impose their arbitrary will upon others, even if they resist. Therefore, racism is an institutionalized mind-set. Historically, humankind, in attempts to explain "what is" and "what ought to be," created religion as a means of reinforcing their existence. Some racial groups anthropologically depicted God in their own image (ethnocentrism) to exploit other human beings. The notion of the "stranger" resulted in social myths and belief systems that set the stage for black vs. white encounters.

This question must be asked: do some whites hate God? Simply because God is the Creator of skin color variety in human beings as well as color in nature (Revelation 4:11). Even in the twenty-first century, the unstated fundamental problem for American society is institutionalized corporate racism. Racism poses some perplexing questions. Why does it exist? What is its social cost? How can it be eradicated? The social pathology of racism invades society like cancer, spreading moral/spiritual bankruptcy, economic waste, occupational mediocrity and political polarization and stagnation. The socio-political state of governmental affairs in America is a classic example of the social costs of exclusivism because racism creates a polarized society. Therefore, racism is birthed in family structures, nurtured in Christian churches and intellectually expressed in our educational institutions. Racism in American society is a culturally based religion, not a godly-centered religion because God hates racism. God created all nations out of one blood. Racism has its mythology (white supremacy), its symbol (physical whiteness), it has its ideology (the exploitation and dehumanization of non-whites) and it is institutionalized simply because the primary qualification is physical whiteness. The ideological foundation of racism is the economic exploitation of non-whites. And, of course, currently there are no racist laws enacted to preclude its existence.

Human societies cannot effectively legislate morality and thought processes. Of course, there are some whites who are caught-up in the mix of the institutionalizing-peer-group immoral mentality. Therefore, racism stems from "idealism and materialism," as manifested in Western socio-religious, philosophical axiology and the rise of the modern capitalist state. In the twenty-first century, given the caste-like economic circumstances of American culture, the color of racism might be green because the American illusion of rags to riches is wishful thinking for some racial and ethnic groups. Racism in America is about privilege without collective moral responsibility that is restricting access to valued resources on the basis of racial and ethnic origin. At its roots, racism (the economic exploitation of non-whites) is a negative idea, and it includes a series of negative correlates, namely (1) whites' negative view of themselves, and (2) blacks' negative view of themselves. Racial oppression in American society is a self-fulfilling prophecy. Whites act as though they are superior and blacks act as though they are inferior because of the negative consequences associated with acting as equals. This is further complicated by the limited avenues of redress for grievances. When one is seeking to be a free will thinking human being in America, resisting the mandated social norm, it results in murder in the name of law and order, unemployment, and physical intimidation.

Racism poses five overriding dilemmas: (1) Loss of national purpose, (2) Economic waste, (3) Occupational mediocrity, (4) Political stagnation, and (5) Political confusion. Human economic exploitation and human community are incompatible concepts. Exclusion invariably costs more than inclusion.

However, there were white English criminals who were given the opportunity to earn their freedom as indentured servants in America. Initially, whites sought to enslave Native Americans but they refused to succumb to the dehumanization of being a slave and of course the consequence was extermination. American and English whites went to Africa in search of slaves and we know the rest of the story because it is American history. Therefore slavery became identified with the color black. Blacks, because of the institutional power differential, can be prejudiced, but not racist. Without a doubt, the color of institutional racism in America is as white as snow and as white as the corporate power structure. Today, there is a black family in the White House, and the White House itself is still painted white, still called The White House, and the corporate power structure is still overwhelmingly white and male.

Racism, in its systematic institutional form, became pervasive with the rise of mercantilism and capitalism. It eventually became crystallized in the western world in order to justify the economic exploitation of individuals with permanent tans. In the conclusion of the matter racism is a white institutional phenomenon simply because too many whites are still in dire need of both personal, peer group influences as well as institutional liberation.

Personal liberation must come first. Whites must culturally "de-whitize" themselves to morally integrate mind and body. By "de-whitize" I mean that that whites must give up their current cultural sense of whiteness (white supremacy), not their biological whiteness, in order to become human. Living beyond physical whiteness is a difficult process because it requires a change of self-concept as well as establishing a system of fairness and consciously living by that system. Living beyond physical whiteness is a difficult process because of peer group influence. That is, because of scientific and technological advances, whites must give up their old white ways and identify with the oppressed and disinherited in the world community. Only then will whites discover the truth about themselves, others, the universe, and, above all, God. Modern negative technology (for example, the nuclear bomb) necessitates the nonviolent resolution of conflict. Unless we as Americans change our thought processes and moral codes of behavior, we will forever remain separate and not equal with the social consequences being that of inconsequential spiritual and physical death.

SELMA

Selma is a historical documentary about American history, not just another movie. It is a documentary that every American should see; especially White Americans. It's mind-boggling that the 87th Academy Award Nomination Committee disrespected the movie Selma. At last, Hollywood has shown its true colors and demonstrated to the world that they cater to whiteness. The Academy Committee lacks moral-intellectual integrity because Hollywood does not really honor talent and creativity but whiteness. Now the world knows who Hollywood is because of the snubbing of the movie Selma. It is a sad day in American society when a documentary film of this historic magnitude is not recognized for its epic contributions to the Civil Rights Movement. Selma has everything individuals love in a movie: drama, suspense, intrigue, and mayhem and violence in all of its raw, racist ugliness.

Twenty-first century America has a Black president and he cannot protect the Civil Rights legislation that President Johnson passed in 1964 and the Voting Rights Act passed in 1965 because of political partisan polarization. For ungodly reasons, the Supreme Court recently stripped the 1965 Voting Rights Act of key provisions.

"For the time will come when they will not endure sound doctrine; but after their own lusts shall heap to themselves teachers, having itching ears; and they shall turn away their ears from the truth, and shall be turned unto fables" (2 Timothy 4:3). The right to vote is the very foundation of American democracy and of course the U.S. Constitution guarantees it. Yet history tells a different story about voting rights for Blacks in America, they have never been free to vote without it being tainted with malice in "the land of the free and the home of the brave."

Make no mistake about it, I am not a professional movie critic, but Selma refueled and triggered memories from my theological training. In 1964, I was a young seminarian at Colgate Rochester Crozer Divinity School (CRCDS) in Rochester, New York. Two weeks before the scheduled Selma March, the seminary invited Malcolm X as a guest lecturer to an annual convocation event. Then, there were only twenty Black seminarians enrolled in CRCDS. I can vividly recall listening to Malcolm X speak the truth about race relations in America. I was in awe listening to Malcolm X as he evoked tears of God-fearing redemption from both Whites and Blacks at a predominantly White seminary. After hearing Malcolm X's speech and watching the media continuously play the horrific images of violence heaped upon the bodies of Americans seeking constitutionally declared voting rights, my classmates and I felt it was time we joined the movement. My fellow classmates, Wilson Fallin, Bobby Joe Saucer, Archie Allen, Edward Jackson, and I jumped in our car and headed to Selma. We remained in Selma for a few days, waiting with expectation to take part in this historic event only to have the March cancelled. As a result of those circumstances, we had no other choice but to return to CRCDS. The March from Selma to Montgomery took place three months later.

Without a doubt, any God-fearing American that views this documentary movie cannot sit through the movie without shedding tears. I cried many times. Viewing Selma reiterates to all Americans, especially Black Americans, who do not exercise their constitutional right to vote, that they do a disservice not only to themselves, but to those individuals who suffered life threating injuries as well as those who died for the right of all Americans to vote. The U.S. Constitution is an almost perfectly written document. It is a document that the world has not seen before—not even the Magna Carta included everyone. However, the legal enforcement of the document is mired in race and ethnicity, social class and gender discrimination.

In the twenty-first century, Blacks must clearly understand the nature of cause and effect that is mirrored in the results of their own behavior regarding their socio-economic plight. Selma clearly demonstrates that the behavior of some Whites has been notoriously ungodly over the almost four hundred years that Blacks have been in America. Some Whites have set a distorted example of Christianity for the world because God hates racism. Hollywood just set a bad example. Of course, this is why we still have institutional racism in the twenty-first century; some whites in high places set a bad examples for others. We may not have racism by law, but racism still exists in individual mindsets and institutional power resources. To be sure, shame, shame, and more shame on Hollywood elites.

Allow me to paraphrase the weeping prophet, Jeremiah: "Oh that my head were waters, and mine eyes a fountain of tears, that I might weep day and night for Hollywood" (Jeremiah 9:1). So where is there hope for the perilous plight Black Americans face even after 400 years of contempt? To conclude the matter, I leave this scripture for all God-fearing Americans to ponder: "What then shall we say to these things? If God is for us, who is against us?" So be it.

At the Table Too Long!

On Sunday, June 25th, 2017, at the 10:30 am service, Covenant Glen UMC hosted its annual worship service honoring community service organizations and public service officials who work tirelessly to make a difference in Metro-Houston. Dr. Robert E. Childress, senior pastor, instituted this special occasion worship service as an expression of thanks to public service professionals. Mayor of the City, Sylvester Turner, delivered a powerful spiritual message concerning public service. I have had conservative leaders acknowledge to me the mayor's positive leadership style. This editorial is a spiritual testimonial concerning the power of the message delivered by the mayor.

First of all, let me say unequivocally that Mayor Turner's leadership style is oriented toward unity of purpose, not political party divisions, as currently is the case in Washington, D.C. In fact, his timely message was truly an inspirational call to unity of purpose for city government. Moreover, everyone deserves a place at the quality of life economic table. Since the Preamble to the U.S. Constitution and the Declaration of Independence, this has been America's clarion call. Mayor Turner emphatically promoted and highlighted inclusion, not exclusion. He also highlighted an important life-altering family experience growing up with a father and mother, and eight siblings. The Turner household was comprised of ten individuals in a home that had a table that could only seat six at a time. Thus, six ate at a time; and, after a while Mayor Turner's father would return to the table, usher the six individuals up, and emphatically declare, "You are spending too much time at the table. It is time to get up. The rest of the family must now eat." Every Houstonian, based upon the U.S. Constitution, deserves a place at the "American Dream Table." The Mayor's use of this analogy was a powerful spiritual depiction of what has taken place, as well as what currently exists, in 2017. For too long, some politicians have not been preparing a place at the table for certain groups. In fact, too many political figures are sitting at the table for personal gain, not public service. Again, it is time for all Houstonians to have a place at the table. In fact, it's time to sh-t or get off the pot.

While the mayor was referencing city government, the analogy is also appropriate to what is going on in America, especially Washington, D.C. "Make America Great Again" is simply coded phraseology for "Make America White-Privilege-Oriented Again." Therefore, the Mayor's analogy clearly speaks to what is going on in Washington, D.C., because individuals with a Trump-like mentality have been at the "American Dream Table" far too long." At the last supper there could have been one too many at the "table": Judas Iscariot. Judas was the betrayer (The Son of Prediction). Lest we as Christians forget,the spiritual message recorded in scripture. "And we know that all things work together for good to them who are the called according to his purpose" (Romans 8: 28). Houstonians, once again, lest we forget, Jesus said, "All that the Father has given me shall come to me; and him that cometh to me I will in no wise cast out" (John 6:37). This is precisely why the exercise of the vote is so important. As a matter of fact, thank God for President Lyndon B. Johnson and the Voting Rights Act of 1965.

Let's be perfectly clear about President Donald J. Trump and stop playing mind-games with our imaginations about the reason(s) why he was elected to the Office of Presidency. After all, working class and poor whites, Christian Evangelicals, and especially White women must now own the spirituality and morality of their vote. They should be embarrassed. Additionally, Black Americans, stop blaming yourselves for not going to the polls to vote or allowing some White men to assassinate the moral and intellectual character of a woman seeking the presidency. The election of Donald J. Trump was not about jobs, it was not about trade agreements, or infrastructure developments, or even healthcare (Obamacare). Plain and simple, it was about race—the Black/White issue. Race in American society still matters. Otherwise, there is no logical explanation for why so many working class and poor, rural Whites embraced a man who has clearly demonstrated over time, in both words and deeds, that he is a self-centered individual, and has mal-nutrition of the brain. More importantly, individuals with a Trump-like mentality have been at the "American Dream Table" far too long. President Trump is hell bent on becoming the most powerful individual on planet earth at the expense of your sons and daughters as well as others. Principle and power are flip-sides of the same coin; therefore, an individual must have principles before acquiring power, otherwise, we have a fool who is admired only by Russia and Israel.

Politics has a clearly defined role in American life, however, the Preamble to the U.S. Constitution and the U.S. Constitution itself states emphatically that every American has a place at the table, yearning to be free with a belief in the principle of "One Man: One Vote." As a result, Mayor Turner's spiritual-message was about inclusion at the table for all Houstonians, not exclusion. The Mayor has a clear-cut understanding of the spiritual-moral principle: "A house divided against itself cannot stand."

Houstonians, "What shall we then say to these things? If God be for us, who can be against us?" (Romans 8:31). Mayor Turner is morally determined that all Houstonians have a place at the table. Moreover, when a man is determined who can stop him? "For as it is written, As I live, saith the Lord, every knee shall bow to me, and every tongue shall confess to God. So then everyone of us shall give account of himself to God. Let us not therefore judge one another anymore, but judge this rather, that no man put a stumbling block or an occasion to fall in his brother's way" (Romans 14:1-13). The message that Mayor Turner delivered on Sunday, June 25th, was spiritually grounded in the Word of God. He used the Good Samaritan story to make the spiritual point of service to others rather than self-serving ego-tripping. Therefore, all Houstonians should "do as much as one can for as many as one can." And, ego-tripping is counter-productive as an option. All of us are called to be Good Samaritans simply because we are our brothers' keeper. "For we are saved by hope: but hope that is seen is not hope: for what a man seeth, why doth he yet hope for. But if we hope for that we see not, then do we with patience wait for it" (Romans 8:24-25). Of course, Blacks have been patiently waiting for almost 400 years for a place at the American Dream table. Our prayer has always been that individuals see the man, not the man's skin color. Selah!

CONCLUSION

President Trump is talking about building an external wall on the Southern border to keep individuals out, when we need to be working on tearing down the internal "spiritual-moral" wall that divides Americans from each other. Remember walls not only keep individuals out, but walls also lock individuals in (The Great Wall of China and the Berlin Wall). President Reagan went to the Berlin Wall and said: "Mr. Gorbachev, tear down this wall". We need "better-ideas, universally-inclusive-policies, and godly tolerance of each other's human rights, and above all, to know where your rights end, and other individuals' rights begins: Building the Kingdom of God on earth as it is in Heaven. If this happens, no walls are needed on either side of the border. For sure, when this happens, then we truly become "our brother's keeper, not our brother's murderer (Cain and Abel story). Seemingly most racists hate groups emerge out of Christian "White" Evangelical churches, and more importantly, pastoral leaders misuse of scriptures as justification for racism and their false teachings. This is why every Christian should: "Study to shew thyself approved of God, a workman that needeth not to be ashamed, rightly dividing the word of truth." (2 Timothy 2: 15).

In fact, given what we know thus far about some "Trump Administration Officials" the campaign slogan, "Lock-Her-Up", is more applicable in relationship to them than Hillary Clinton. In fact, they should be behind prison walls, and absolutely, not behind White House Walls. Praise God, most Americans who voted in the 2016 Presidential election knew that businessman Donald J. Trump should not be in The White House. President Trump lost the popular vote by almost 3 million votes.   However, the "Electoral-College-System" dictated otherwise!

President Trump has proven himself to be a first-class "buffoon" that will say anything as well as do anything. And, above all, Trump's "bellicose" language-style is dangerously ignorant for American society as well as the world community. America is a citizen-civilian-oriented democratic nation state; not a military dictatorship. Therefore, military action is always the last resort. And, seemingly thirty-four-percent of America's voting population is in wholehearted agreement with his insane approach to Presidential Governance and others "go-along-to-get-along". However, silence is ungodly, because silence is consent. God-fearing individuals must always speak truth to power no matter the consequences.

Moreover, the hatred and devilish desire of President Trump and some Republican Party Officials to destroy the "legacy-reality" of President Barack Obama, a Black man, as President, and above all, his family residing in The White House has fueled the insanity of racism. This was done to the Civil Rights Legacy of President Lyndon B. Johnson, a Southerner, who was one of America's greatest Presidents of valor. So much so that it is no accident of American history that the driving personality behind the "Birther-Movement" is now President of these United States of America, a "lying-entertainment-performer", not a man of valor. Moreover, it appears as though this is what many

Americans, at least one-third of the White electorate wanted, because they have a "can't get over it mentality". Forget: Hell No". Hence, a large percentage of Trump voters were racially motivated by the past: (Southern-Mentality-Can't-Get-Over-It). America, to be sure, God still rules the world. "For we must all appear before the judgement seat of Christ; that every one may receive the things done in his body, according to that he hath done, whether it be good or bad." (2 Corinthians 5: 10).

Many Trump supporters wanted "mentally-challenged" leadership, because they feared cultural displacement. Shame! Shame! Shame! Moreover, it seems as though President Trump is "hell-bent" on starting a war in order to remain in the White House, a place that he has called a "DUMP". Even though in his "narrow-non-historical-mind" the White House is a "DUMP", he was willing to trash the moral character of (16) other Republican opponents in order that he might live there! Shame! Shame! Shame! President Trump's language style and behavior demeans the Office of President, simply because he is an emotional thinker that loves CHAOS and CONFLICT.

On August 12th, 2017 America's under-current "racial-divide-original-sin-problem" erupted in a violent "terroristic" manner in Charlottesville, Virginia. Seemingly there are some Whites who invariably want Blacks as well as other minorities to apologize to them for being Black or brown, and therefore, they will not have to apologize to God for being racist, especially since God hates racism. The August 12th violent display of racist hatred was the culmination of the Republican Party's 2016 primary election, and the subsequent election of Donald J. Trump dating back to Goldwater 1964 and the

Republican Party's Southern strategy employed by President Richard M. Nixon. Subsequently, President Trump has felt embolden, so much so, that he brought the likes of ALT-Right-Stephen Bannon, racist-combative Stephen Miller, and Nazi sympathizer Dr. Sebastian Gorka into the White House along with Kelly-Anne Conway as the Amen-Alternative-Fact-Chieftain, and Sarah Huckabee Sanders as the spokesperson for Presidential confusion.

The insanity of racism was clearly on display in the actions of James Alex Fields. Mr. Fields lives in the greatest society on planet earth. The System works for the System, and the System was created by White men for White men. Mr. Fields with all of the privileges that are enthroned in that status is spiritually unconscious about himself, so he had to blame some else for his "personal" shortcomings. Just as The Alt-Right, Nazis, and other White Supremacists cannot accept the reality of who they are. Instead of Mr. Fields preparing to return to college as a junior, he was preparing to drive from Ohio to Virginia to participate in a vulgar "public" display of White supremacy all in the name of President Trump. This fellow Americans is the epitome of the insanity of "RACISM". There is absolutely nothing; except his own hatred of self and others that is preventing Mr. Fields from becoming a successful citizen or experiencing success in life (doctor, lawyer, Engineer or CEO) in American society.

The Grand Dragon of the KKK, David Duke, emphatically declared: "We are determined to take our country back". Question: Take it back from whom? Take it back from Native American Indians; we already accomplished that through genocidal war! Take it back from the North whose only desire was to preserve the UNION: United States of

America. It cannot be take it back from Black Americans? I don't think so! Because it was through Black slave labor that America was built. Of course, all that Black America has is the sacred promise of the Preamble to U.S. Constitution and The Articles of the Constitution.

It is time for America to learn from its "morally-conflicted" historical past, and make-up for the mistakes of the past. Christian Right Evangelical pastors you can play an important spiritual pastoral healing role in American society simply by preaching "God's Spiritual Truth" based upon Biblical doctrines, and stop preaching and teaching "White-Privilege-Isms" from pulpits. Apparently, Christian Evangelical pastors are sowing spiritual seeds of discord in White families. Racial hatred is a taught and learned social experience. In fact, racial hatred is an unnatural phenomenon, which in turn, is taught and nurtured in families, Christian churches, civic organizations, and society in general. Hence, hatred does not call individuals into being. LOVE (GOD) is the foundation of human life, because God is love. American society, hear and heed this, Whites have "absolute" power authority control over every "socio-economic" facet of American society, and absolute power, corrupts absolutely. Apparently, White racists want to take the reins of power from other Whites. The question is WHY? Of course, there is nothing wrong with being ambitious, but there is something wrong with being vicious "physically" because of your ambition, and above all, "spiritual-moral" ignorance.

Since June of 2016, President Trump has been seeking to defend the indefensible this is why it took 48 hours for him to "half-heartedly" appease America, and smoothed over condemnation of the "racist-oriented-domestic-terrorism" that occurred in Charlottesville, Virginia. Without a doubt, America needs a President that knows and understands what to say, and above all, when to say it, because "Death and life are in the tongue: and they that love it shall eat the fruit thereof." Selah!

9 781984 311498